Practice Problems for FINANCIAL ALGEBRA
Advanced Algebra with Financial Applications

Practice Problems for FINANCIAL ALGEBRA
Advanced Algebra with Financial Applications

Second Edition

Robert Gerver

Richard Sgroi

Australia • Brazil • Mexico • Singapore • United Kingdom • United States

Practice Problems for Financial Algebra: Advanced Algebra with Financial Applications, Second Edition

Robert Gerver and Richard Sgroi

SVP, GM Skills & Global Product Management: Jonathan Lau

Product Manager: Nicole Robinson

Senior Director, Development: Marah Bellegarde

Senior Product Development Manager: Juliet Steiner

Senior Content Developer: Darcy M. Scelsi

Product Assistant: Deborah Handy

Vice President, Marketing Services: Jennifer Ann Baker

Marketing Manager: Sebastian Andino

Senior Production Director: Wendy Troeger

Production Director: Andrew Crouth

Senior Content Project Manager: Glenn Castle

Senior Art Director: Jack Pendleton

Technology Project Manager: Mary Colleen Liburdi

Media Editor: Melina Iacovone

Cover image(s): Cover app icons created by Michael Gerver

Library of Congress Control Number: 2016958582

ISBN: 978-1-3372-7182-0

Cengage Learning
20 Channel Center Street
Boston, MA 02210
USA

Cengage Learning is a leading provider of customized learning solutions with employees residing in nearly 40 different countries and sales in more than 125 countries around the world. Find your local representative at www.cengage.com.

Cengage Learning products are represented in Canada by Nelson Education, Ltd.

To learn more about Cengage Learning, visit **www.cengage.com**

Purchase any of our products at your local college store or at our preferred online store **www.cengagebrain.com**

Notice to the Reader

Printed in the United States of America

Print Number: 04   Print Year: 2017

Table of Contents

1-1   Discretionary and Essential Expenses

Exercises

1. For most people, the cost of a subscription to streaming music services is definitely a discretionary expense. Marshal researched subscription costs and found the following rates for streaming services:

   $10/mo., $6/mo., $33/year, $3/mo., $5/mo., $10/mo., $10/mo., $4/mo., $12/mo., $60/year

   a. In order to analyze the data, the subscription rates must cover the same time period. Change the yearly rates to monthly rates.

   b. What is the mean monthly subscription fee? Round your answer to the nearest cent.

   c. What is the median monthly subscription fee?

   d. What is the mode monthly membership fee?

2. Carla is a carpenter. She wants to purchase new high-quality tools for her business. She found the following prices for the exact same set of tools from various sellers:

   $6,700 $7,450 $8,000 $7,600 $7,450 $8,200 $7,210

   a. What is the mean price? Round your answer to the nearest cent.

   b. What is the median price?

   c. What is the mode price?

3. According to the Bureau of Economic Analysis, the monthly percentage change of disposable income in the United States over the course of a year from February to February was reported as follows:

   0.3%   0%   0.6%   0.5%   0.5%   0.4%   0.3%   0.2%   0.3%   0.2%   0.3%   0.4%   0.2%

   a. What was the mean percent change over this period? Round your answer to the nearest hundredth of a percent.

   b. What was the median percent change over this period.

   c. From January to February of the second year, a 0.2% change in disposable income was reported. If the January amount was 12.43 billion dollars, what would the February amount be? Round your answer to two decimal places.

4. In their brochure, AutoNation Career School estimated the average discretionary personal expenses for a student attending to be $2,850. Martin is a student and feels that the amount is too high. He polled his co-students and made a list of their actual school year expenses:

$2,500 $2,600 $3,000 $3,200 $2,700 $2,900 $2,850

   a. What is the mean of these students' personal expenses? Round your answer to the nearest cent.

   b. How does that average compare with the estimate?

   c. What would Martin's actual personal expenses for that school year have to be so that his amount and his co-students' amounts together would have an average of $2,850?

Use the following table to answer questions 5–8.

Monthly Cell Phone Bills

Jan	Feb	Mar	Apr	May	June	July	Aug	Sept	Oct	Nov	Dec
x_1	x_2	x_3	x_4	x_5	x_6	x_7	x_8	x_9	x_{10}	x_{11}	x_{12}
$83	$86	$78	$82	$95	$87	$90	$76	$88	$82	$83	$71

5. Write the formula for the mean cell phone bill for the entire year using sigma notation and determine that mean. Round your answer to the nearest cent.

6. Write the formula for the mean cell phone bill for the last six months of the year using sigma notation and determine that mean. Round your answer to the nearest cent.

7. Write the formula for the mean cell phone bill from March to September using sigma notation and determine that mean. Round your answer to the nearest cent.

8. Write the sigma notation mean formula for the 3 consecutive month period that would have the highest mean of the year.

Name _____ Date _____

Use the following table to answer questions 9–11.

Janet attends State University and lives in an on-campus dorm suite with 5 friends. They share the cost of the monthly upgraded cable bill for their suite. Below is a listing of the bills for their freshman year.

Monthly Cable Bill

Sept	Oct	Nov	Dec	Jan	Feb	Mar	Apr	May
x_1	x_2	x_3	x_4	x_5	x_6	x_7	x_8	x_9
$65	$70	$84	$76	$50	$80	$78	$78	$67

9. Round the following value $\dfrac{1}{9}\sum\limits_{i=1}^{9} x_i$ to the nearest dollar.

   Interpret the answer in the context of the problem.

10. Round the following value $\dfrac{1}{4}\sum\limits_{i=1}^{4} x_i$ to the nearest dollar.

    Interpret the answer in the context of the problem.

11. Write the sigma notation mean formula for the second semester beginning in February and determine that semester average rounded to the nearest dollar.

12. The New York Premier Theater is hosting a concert at which all proceeds will go to the charity. The seating chart is shown here:

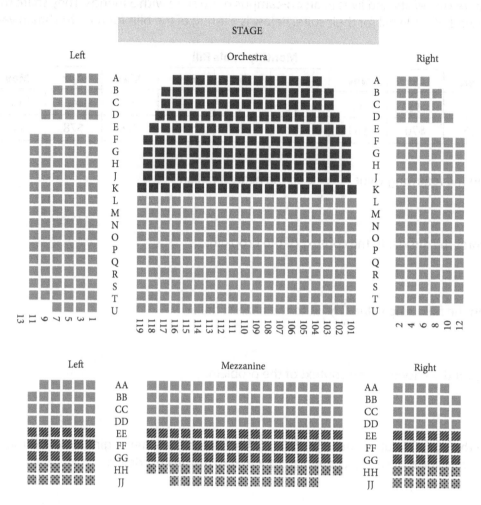

The seating options for the color-coded seats are priced as follows:

▦ Rear Mezzanine 54 seats, each at $150

▨ Middle Mezzanine 87 seats, each at $200

▨ Front Mezzanine and Orchestra 512 seats, each at $300

■ Front and Center Orchestra 167 seats, each at $500

a. Construct a frequency distribution with column headings "Seat Type", "Price", and "Number of Seats".

b. If all of the seats were sold for this concert, what would be the total amount to be donated to charity?

c. Determine the mean, median, and mode seat prices. Round to the nearest cent.

13. Although companies would like consumers to believe that identity theft protection is an essential expense, in reality it is discretionary. A consumer organization compared the monthly costs of similar identity theft protection plans on the market and published the following list:

$14.99 $12.75 $14.99 $14.99 $9.99 $25 $25 $10 $14.99 $10 $20 $10 $20

$14.99 $10 $25 $20 $12 $14.99 $25 $25 $20 $12.75 $10 $9.99

a. Write the formula for the mean in sigma notation and use it to calculate the mean monthly plan price. Round your answer to the nearest cent.

b. Construct a frequency distribution for the data.

c. Use the frequency distribution to determine the mean. Round to the nearest cent.

d. Use the frequency distribution to determine the median and the mode.

1-2 Travel Expenses

Exercises

1. A certain rail company uses a method called demand pricing for setting the prices of their seats. The price per seat starts at a fixed amount. As the train starts to fill up, the prices gradually increase. A consumer watchdog agency selected a random coach car on a train traveling between New York and Philadelphia. They asked each traveler for the price paid for the seat. The following is the result of their survey.

a. Extend the graph by adding a cumulative frequency column. Calculate the 6 entries for that column and answer the questions below.

b. How many passengers paid a fare at or below $45?

c. How many passengers paid a fare at or above $70?

Price	Frequency	Cumulative Frequency
$39	12	
$45	17	
$55	14	
$70	7	
$88	5	
$107	4	

d. How many passengers paid a fare that was at least $45 and at most $88?

2. Use the table in problem 1 to answer these questions.

a. Add a relative frequency column. Calculate the relative frequencies. Round each to the nearest thousandth.

b. Which ticket prices have a relative frequency greater than 0.2 and less than 0.3?

c. Interpret the relative frequency for the $88 ticket price in terms of a percent.

Name _____ Date _____

3. Many people travel to Florida to visit the popular theme parks there. The table below lists yearly attendance at one of those parks for 6 consecutive years.

Year	Attendance in millions
2009	17.3
2010	16.97
2011	17.14
2012	17.54
2013	18.59
2014	19.33

Use the table to answer the questions below.

a. Add a "Relative Frequency" column to the table and determine all of the entries in that column. Round your entries to three decimal places.

b. Add a "Cumulative Frequency" column to the table and determine all of the entries in that column. Express your answer in millions to two decimal places.

c. Add a "Relative Cumulative Frequency" column to the table and determine all of the entries in that column. Round your entries to three decimal places.

d. What was the average monthly number of visitors in millions attending this theme park over this 6-year period? Round to the nearest tenth of a million.

e. What was the median number of park visitors?

f. Use your completed chart. What percent of the total number of visitors attended in 2014?

g. Use your chart. Approximately what percent of all people entering the park did so in 2009, 2010, and 2011 combined? Where would you find this information in your chart?

4. Jim lives in San Francisco and attends school at a university in New York City. He wants to travel home for his sister's wedding next month and has researched round trip airfares. The table lists all available itineraries with fares below $400.

RT Fares	Frequency	Rel. Freq.	Cum. Freq.	Re. Cum. Freq.
$326	2	0.024	2	0.024
$336	10	0.119	12	0.143
$340	2	0.024	14	0.167
$344	4	b.	18	0.214
$350	5	0.060	23	f.
$357	9	0.107	d.	0.381
$366	15	0.179	47	0.560
$371	3	0.036	50	0.595
$376	2	c.	52	0.619
$379	6	0.071	58	g.
$384	17	0.202	e.	0.893
$392	9	0.107	84	1.000
Total	a.			

Use the table to determine the missing values a–g.

5. Four car rental prices were quoted for a 1-day rental. The frequencies are listed. Let Y represent the frequency of the $83 price quote. Use the information shown in the chart to write algebraic expressions for the entries labeled a–e.

1-day Car Rental	Frequency	Relative Frequency	Cumulative Frequency	Relative Cumulative Frequency
$65	4			
$72	2	b.		
$83	Y	c.		
$100	3		d.	e.
Total	a.			

Name _____ Date _____

6. Tesa lives in a major city. Her employer pays for her round trip taxicab fare from home to work each day. She must keep receipts for each trip and turn them in at the end of each month for reimbursement. The fares are based on distance and time so they change each day due to traffic, construction, weather, and other factors. Below is an ordered list of her round-trip fares for the 23 workdays in August.

23.00   23.00   24.25   24.25   24.25   24.25   24.25   24.75

25.50   25.50   25.50   25.50   25.50   25.50   25.60   25.75

25.80   25.80   25.80   25.90   25.90   25.95   25.95

   a. Find the percentile rank for a fare of $25.50. Interpret your results.

   b. Find the percentile rank for a fare of $25.90. Interpret your results.

   c. Based on your answers to parts a and b of this problem, which fare would have a percentile rank of about 70%?

7. The table below lists all train fares quoted from Washington, DC, to Philadelphia, PA, on a given day.

   a. Write an algebraic expression for the percentile rank of $42.

   b. Write an algebraic expression for the percentile rank of $48.

   c. Write an algebraic expression for the percentile rank of $55.

Cost to Airport	Frequency
$42	a
$48	b
$55	c
$68	d
$90	e
$109	f

   d. Write an algebraic expression for the percentile rank of $68.

   e. Write an algebraic expression for the percentile rank of $90.

   f. Write an algebraic expression for the percentile rank of $109.

1-3 Entertainment Expenses

Exercises

1. Following are the prices of 12 tickets listed on the *Ticket Racket* ticket broker site for a Bruce Springsteen concert.

   $75, 120, 120, 145, 150, 150, 150, 175, 175, 200, 225, 275

   Round your answers to the nearest hundredth.

   a. What is the mean ticket price?   **b.** What is the median ticket price?

   c. What is the mode ticket price?   **d.** What is the range?

   e. What is the variance?   **f.** What is the standard deviation?

2. The variance of a distribution is 50. What is the standard deviation, rounded to the nearest thousandth?

3. The following is a list of Relay for Life donations given by several community businesses in the Maple Glen High School vicinity.

   $10, $50, $100, $100, $100, $120, $120, $125, $150, $150, $250.

   Round your answers to the nearest hundredth.

   a. What is the mean donation amount?   **b.** What is the range?

   c. What is the variance?   **d.** What is the standard deviation?

4. Airline fares can vary greatly, even from the same carrier within the same day. The following are fares from New York to Burbank, CA, over the past week.

   $430, $567, $334, $701, $424, $555, $890, $455, $450, $1,122

   What is the standard deviation for this distribution? Round your answers to the nearest dollar.

5. The distribution of cell phone bills for families in Smithtown North High School has mean $183 and standard deviation 11. At Smithtown South High School, the mean is $181 and the standard deviation is 21. Which distribution is more spread out?

6. The following is a distribution of the number of individual song downloads made by students in Arlington High School's Acoustic Café Club last year.

12, 11, 21, 43, 23, 51, 19, 22, 88, 60

   a. Find the mean number of downloads per club member.

   b. If each club member increased their downloads by 6, what happens to the mean?

   c. If each club member multiplies their downloads by 3, what happens to the mean?

   d. Find the median number of downloads per club member.

   e. If each club member increased their downloads by 6, what happens to the median?

   f. If each club member multiplies their downloads by 3, what happens to the median?

   g. Find the range of the distribution.

   h. If each club member increased their downloads by 6, what happens to the range?

   i. If each club member multiplies their downloads by 3, what happens to the range?

   j. Find the standard deviation of the original distribution to the nearest thousandth.

   k. If each club member increased their downloads by 6, what happens to the standard deviation?

   l. If each club member multiplies their downloads by 3, what happens to the standard deviation?

7. Look at the original data in problem 6. Suppose the number 60 was changed to 600 and the rest of the numbers remained the same.

   a. Would the mean be affected?   b. Would the median be affected?

   c. Would the range be affected?   d. Would the standard deviation be affected?

8. A high school theater production had an admission price of $10. During the show, 876 people paid to enter.

   a. What is the range of the distribution of admission fees?

   b. What is the standard deviation of the distribution of admission fees?

   c. If the standard deviation of a distribution is 0, must all of the data be the same number? Explain.

9. A class of 31 students averaged 82 on a recent exam. Two students were absent and took the exam the next day. The two students averaged 88 on their exam. What was the average for the entire class, including the two students who took the test one day later?

10. The number of cars owned by households in the Lakebridge Condominium Complex is shown in the table.

Number of Cars Owned	Frequency, f	$x_i f$	$x_i - \bar{x}$	$(x_i - \bar{x})^2$	$(x_i - \bar{x})^2 f$
0	22	c.	h.	l.	p.
1	43	d.	i.	m.	q.
2	52	e.	j.	n.	r.
3	3	f.	k.	o.	s.
TOTAL	n = 120	g.			t.

   a. Find the mean number of cars owned per household.

   b. Fill in the missing entries in the table to the nearest hundredth.

   c. Find the standard deviation of the distribution to the nearest hundredth.

12. A distribution consists of 30 scores of 10 and 30 scores of 20. Find the ratio of the range to the standard deviation.

13. Create a distribution of five numbers that has range 10, maximum score 20, and mean 12.

1-4 Vacation Expenses

Exercises

1. A travel agency did a survey and found that the average local family spends $1,900 on a summer vacation. The distribution is normally distributed with standard deviation $390.

    a. What percent of the families took vacations that cost under $1,500? Round to the nearest percent.

    b. What percent of the families took vacations that cost over $2,800? Round to the nearest percent.

    c. Find the amount a family would have spent to be the 60th percentile. Round to the nearest dollar.

2. A distribution is normal with mean 60 and standard deviation 8. Find the area of each of the following shaded regions to four decimal places.

    a.

    b.

    c.

    d.

3. A family of two adults and two children on vacation in the United States will pay an average of $247 per day for food and lodging with a standard deviation of $60 per day, according to a recent survey by a national travel association.

    a. Find, to the nearest hundredth, the *z*-score for $150 for vacation food and lodging expenses.

    b. If a vacationer had a *z*-score of 2.1, what were their daily expenses for food and lodging?

    c. If the data is normally distributed, find the percent of these vacationers who spent less than $307 per day.

    d. What is the variance?

    e. What is the mean expense for food and lodging for a 7-day vacation?

4. The Vacation Times website rates recreational vehicle campgrounds using integers from 0 to 15. Last year they rated over 1,000 campsites. The ratings were normally distributed with mean 7.6 and standard deviation 1.7.

    a. How high would a campsite's rating have to be for it to be considered in the top 10% of rated campsites? Round to the nearest hundredth.

    b. Find the *z*-score for a rating of 5. Round to the nearest hundredth.

    c. Find the percentile for a rating of 7.5. Round to the nearest percent.

    d. A campsite had a *z*-score of 2. What was its rating?

5. A certain amusement park ride requires riders to be at least 48 inches tall. If the heights of children in a summer camp are normally distributed with mean 52 and standard deviation 2.5, how many of the 140 campers will be allowed on the ride? Round to the nearest integer.

6. What *z*-score on the Normal Curve table has an area of 0.8849 to its left?

7. What *z*-score on the Normal Curve table has an area of 0.6808 to its right?

Name _____   Date _____

8. *Travel Times Journal* found that the average per person cost of a 10-day trip along the Pacific coast, per person, is $1,015. This includes transportation, food, lodging, and entertainment.

   a. If the data is normally distributed with standard deviation $198, find the percent of vacationers who spent less than $1,200 per day. Round to the nearest hundredth of a percent.

   b. Find the per-day expense for one of these travelers who had a *z*-score of –1.6.

   c. A *Bargain Times Vacation Blog* writer claimed to have done this vacation for a cost of $710 per person. What percentile is represented by $710? Round to the nearest hundredth of a percentile.

9. The school nurse at West Side Elementary School weighs all of the 230 children by the end of September. She finds that the students' weights are normally distributed with mean 98 and standard deviation 16. After compiling all the data, she realizes that the scale was incorrect—it was reading two pounds over the actual weight. She adjusts the records for all 230 children.

   a. What is the effect of the correction on the mean?

   b. What is the correct mean?

   c. What is the effect of the correction on the standard deviation?

10. During a recent summer month, airfares from Miami, FL, to Seattle, WA, were normally distributed with mean $760 and standard deviation $136.

   a. Sketch a normal curve and shade in the interval below $500.

   b. Find the *z*-score for a fare of $500.

   c. What percent of the airfares were below $500?

   d. The lowest 5% of airfares represents a real bargain. What airfare represents the 5th percentile?

   e. What percent of the airfares were below the median?

1-5 | Personal Expenses

Exercises

1. Each month you have $200 automatically deposited from your checking account into a discretionary savings account. Your plan is to leave the money in this account for the next 10 years in order to use the total at that time at your discretion. A scatter plot shows the number of months that have passed and the amount in your discretionary spending account each month. The explanatory x-variable is the number of months that have passed. The response y-variable is the amount in your savings account. Is there a positive or negative correlation? Explain.

2. Determine if the scatter plot below depicts a positive correlation or a negative correlation.

3. Describe each of the following correlation coefficients using the terms strong, moderate, or weak and negative or positive.

   a. $r = -0.19$ **b.** $r = -0.93$ **c.** $r = 0.57$

   d. $r = 0.0999$ **e.** $r = -0.97$ **f.** $r = -0.45$

4. Lori created a scatter plot where the explanatory variable was the side of a square, and the response variable was the perimeter of the square. Is the data positively or negatively correlated? Explain.

5. In each situation of bivariate data there is causation, so the variables can be named explanatory and response variables. Identify each explanatory variable and response variable.

   a. number of days worked, amount earned

   b. amount earned in the year, income taxes paid

   c. temperature, number of swimmers at the beach

   d. price of a dress, number of dresses sold

6. MoviePlay is an online movie rental service. They have a sliding price list based upon the popularity of the movies. The table below shows the rentals by price category for the month of September. Let x represent the price and y represent the number of movies rented at that price.

Price	# of rentals
5.99	800
4.99	1,000
3.99	1,200
2.99	1,380
1.99	1,672
0.99	1,903

a. Examine the data without drawing a scatter plot. Describe any trends you see.

b. Draw a scatter plot. Describe the correlation.

c. Based on this information, how many rentals might be anticipated if the company instituted a new price category of $6.99. Explain your reasoning.

Name_____ Date_____

7. The table below lists the percentage of households with an income of $100,000 or more that spent money on fitness-related activities over the course of one year as reported by statista.com.

Fitness Spending in dollars (d)	Percent of households with an income of $100,00 or more
0	53.7%
$0 < d < 250$	17.8%
$250 \leq d < 500$	12.5%
$500 \leq d < 1000$	8.4%
$1000 \leq d < 2000$	5%
$2000 \leq d < 3000$	1.5%
$3000 \leq d < 5000$	0.7%
$5000 \leq d < 10,000$	0.2%

a. Without making a scatter plot, what trend do you see in the data.

b. Draw a scatter plot. Let x represent the spending interval number ($x = 1$ when d = 0, $x = 2$ when $0 < d < 250$, $x = 3$ when $250 \leq d < 500$ etc.) Describe the correlation.

c. Based on the trend, scatter plot, and correlation, what might you predict the percentage to be for households that had $10,000 to $15,000 fitness-related expenses?

8. In Application 6 for section 1-5 in the textbook, you were given the following table about discretionary personal back-to-school personal expenses.

a. Determine the linear regression equation that best fits the data presented in the table. Let x represent the year and y represent the back-to-school spending amount per family. Round numbers to the nearest hundredth.

b. Determine the correlation coefficient for the bivariate data. Round to the nearest hundredth. Interpret that correlation coefficient.

c. Use the linear regression equation to predict the spending amount in 2016. Round your answer to the nearest cent.

Year	Back to School Spending in Dollars per Family
2004	$483.28
2005	$443.77
2006	$527.08
2007	$563.49
2008	$594.24
2009	$548.72
2010	$606.40
2011	$603.63
2012	$688.82
2013	$634.79
2014	$669.28
2015	$630.36

d. Rather than using the actual year values, x could have represented the year number where $x = 1$ represents 2004, $x = 2$ represents 2005, and so on. Replace the year numbers for x in your list. Determine the regression line using this bivariate data set. Do you get the same regression equation as in part a?

e. What similarities and differences do you see in the two regression equations? Explain.

f. Use the second linear regression equation to predict the spending for 2016. What x-value will you use in this case to represent 2016?

9. The Super Bowl is a big money-making and money-spending event. The discretionary spending amounts on Super Bowl weekends are in the billions of dollars. Examine the chart below that lists TV viewer numbers and Super Bowl weekend-related expenses by year.

Year	TV Viewers in millions	Money Spent in billions
2007	93.18	8.71
2008	92.45	9.47
2009	98.73	9.56
2010	106.48	8.87
2011	111	10.15
2012	111.3	11.02
2013	108.4	12.28
2014	111.5	12.37
2015	114.4	14.31
2016	111.9	15.53

a. Determine the linear regression equation where x represents the year number ($x = 1$ represents 2007, $x = 2$ represents 2008, etc.) and y represents the money spent. Round all numbers to the nearest thousandth. What is the correlation coefficient? What can you infer from the coefficient?

b. Determine the linear regression equation where x represents the number of TV viewers and y represents the money spent. Round all numbers to the nearest thousandth. What is the correlation coefficient? What can you infer from the differences between this coefficient and the one found in part a?

2-1 Checking Accounts

Exercises

1. Mitchell has a balance of $1,200 in his First State Bank checking account. He deposits a $387.89 paycheck, a $437.12 dividend check, and a personal check for $250 into his account. He wants to receive $400 in cash. How much will he have in his account after the transaction?

2. Meg has a total of d dollars in her checking account. She makes a cash deposit of c dollars and a deposit of three checks each worth s dollars. She would like e dollars in cash from this transaction. She has enough money in her account to cover the cash received. Express her new checking account balance after the transaction as an algebraic expression.

3. Neal deposited a $489.50 paycheck, an x dollar stock dividend check, a y dollar rebate check, and $85 cash into his checking account. His original account balance was w dollars. Assume each check clears. Write an expression for the balance in his account after the deposits?

4. Elaine has m dollars in her checking account. On December 8, she deposited $1,200, r dollars, and $568.90. She also cashed a check for t dollars and one for $73.70. Write an algebraic expression that represents the amount of money in her account after the transactions.

5. Del and Jen have a joint checking account. Their balance at the beginning of October was $6,238.67. During the month they made deposits totaling d dollars, wrote checks totaling $1,459.98, paid a maintenance fee of z dollars, and earned b dollars in interest on the account. Write an algebraic expression that represents the balance at the end of the month?

6. New Merrick Bank charges a $21-per-check overdraft protection fee. On June 5, Lewis had $989.00 in his account. Over the next few days, the following checks were submitted for payment at his bank: June 6, $875.15, $340.50, and $450.63; June 7, $330; and June 8, $560.00.

   a. How much will he pay in overdraft protection fees?

   b. How much will he owe the bank after June 8?

7. Dean has a checking account at City Center Bank. During the month of April, he made deposits totaling $2,458.52 and wrote checks totaling $789.23. He paid a maintenance fee of $25 and earned $3.24 in interest. His balance at the end of the month was $4,492.76. What was the balance at the beginning of April?

8. Bellrose Bank charges a monthly maintenance fee of $17 and a check-writing fee of $0.05 per check. Last year, Patricia wrote 445 checks from her account at Bellrose. What was the total of all fees she paid on that account last year?

9. Create a check register for the transactions listed.

  a. Your balance on 1/5 is $822.67.

  b. You write check 1076 on 1/6 for $600.00 to Excel Health Club.

  c. You deposit a paycheck for $227.45 on 1/11.

  d. You deposit a $50 rebate check on 1/15.

  e. On 1/16, you begin writing a donation check to Clothes for Kids but make an error and have to void the check. You write the very next check for $100 to this organization.

  f. On 1/20, you withdraw $200 from the ATM at the mall. The company owning the ATM charges you $3.50 and your bank charges you $2.50 for the ATM transaction.

  g. On 1/21, you made a debit card purchase at Stacy's Store for $134.87.

  h. Your friend gave you the $1,300 he owed you and you deposit it on 1/22.

  i. You write the next check on 1/23 to iBiz for $744.24 for a new computer.

  j. You deposit your paycheck for $227.45 on 1/23.

  k. On 1/24, you withdraw $50 from the ATM affiliated with your bank. There are no fees.

  l. On 1/24, you write the next check for $75.00 to iTel Wireless.

  m. On 1/25, you write a check for $120 concert tickets to Ticket King.

NUMBER OR CODE	DATE	TRANSACTION DESCRIPTION	PAYMENT AMOUNT	✓	FEE	DEPOSIT AMOUNT	$ BALANCE
	1/5	Balance	$				822.67
1076	1/6	Excel Health Club	600.00				222.67
	1/11	Paycheck deposit				227.45	450.12
	1/15	Rebate check				50.00	500.12
1077	1/16	VOID					500.12
1078	1/16	Clothes for Kids	100.00				400.12
	1/20	ATM withdrawal – mall	200.00		6.00		194.12
	1/21	Stacy's Store (debit)	134.87				59.25
	1/22	Deposit from friend				1,300.00	1,359.25
1079	1/23	iBiz computer	744.24				615.01
	1/23	Paycheck deposit				227.45	842.46
	1/24	ATM withdrawal – bank	50.00				792.46
1080	1/24	iTel Wireless	75.00				717.46
1081	1/25	Ticket King	120.00				597.46

10. Create a check register for the transactions listed.

    a. Your balance on 2/25 is $769.22.

    b. On 2/25, you write check 747 for $18 to Steve Smith.

    c. On 2/27, you deposit your paycheck in the amount of $450.80.

    d. Your grandparents send you a check for $50, which you deposit into your account on 2/28.

    e. On 3/2 you write a check to North State College for $300.00 and another check to Middle Island Auto Parts for $120.65.

    f. Later in the day on 3/2 you write two more checks: Metro Transit for $85.00 and Bling's Department Store for $58.76.

    g. On 3/3, at Border Barns Books, as you write the next check for $105.85, you make a mistake and void that check. You pay with the next available check in your checkbook.

    h. On 3/5, you deposit a rebate check for $425 into your checking account.

    i. On 3/8, you pay your car insurance with an e-check to AllFarm Insurance for $521.30.

    j. On 3/10, you withdraw $300 from the ATM. There is a $4.50 charge for using the ATM.

    k. On 3/11, you deposit your paycheck in the amount of $450.00.

    l. On 3/12, you use your debit card to make three purchases at Sports Master: $88.91, $23.50, and $100.70.

    m. On 3/13, you transfer $1,000 from your savings account into your checking account.

    n. On 3/13, you write a check to Empire Properties for your first month's rent in your new apartment in the amount of $820.00.

    o. On 3/15, you use your debit card to purchase a $150.00 microwave at Kitchen Supply.

Name _____ Date _____

(Transactions are listed on the previous page.)

NUMBER OR CODE	DATE	TRANSACTION DESCRIPTION	PAYMENT AMOUNT	✓	FEE	DEPOSIT AMOUNT	$ BALANCE
			$				

2-2 Reconcile a Bank Statement

Exercises

1. On the back of Elise's monthly statement, she listed the following outstanding withdrawals: #123, $76.09; #117, $400; #130, $560.25; debit card, $340.50; and #138, $83.71. She also determined that a deposit for $500 and another for $328.90 are outstanding. Using these outstanding transactions, what adjustment will have to be made to her statement balance?

2. Pina filled out the following information on the back of her monthly statement:

Ending balance from statement	$1,139.78
Deposits outstanding	+ $280.67
Total of checks outstanding	– $656.91
Revised statement balance	$_____
Balance from checkbook	$763.54

   Find Pina's revised statement balance. Does her account reconcile?

3. Tasha filled out the following information on the back of her bank statement:

Ending balance from statement	$764.22
Deposits outstanding	+ $387.11
Total of checks outstanding	– $455.32
Revised statement balance	$_____
Balance from checkbook	$669.01

   Find Tasha's revised statement balance. Does her account reconcile?

4. Lenny opened a checking account last month. Today he received his first statement. The statement listed five deposits and 24 checks that cleared. Lenny's check register shows nine outstanding checks. How many checks has Lenny written since the account was opened?

5. Arden's checking account charges a $21 monthly maintenance fee with no per-check fee. He wants to switch to a different account with a fee of 18 cents per check and a $15 monthly maintenance fee. The following information is about his last five monthly statements.

Month	Number of Checks on Statement	Month	Number of Checks on Statement	Month	Number of Checks on Statement
Feb	24	Mar	37	Apr	35
May	33	June	41		

   a. What is the mean number of checks Arden wrote per month during the last five months?

   b. About how much should Arden expect to pay per month for the new checking account?

   c. What advice would you give Arden?

6. Below you will find Mitch West's monthly statement and his check register. Use them to complete parts a–e in his checking account summary. Does his account reconcile?

Mitch West
23 Sycamore Lane
Benridge, NY 10506

ACCOUNT NUMBER: 456213-A232
STATEMENT PERIOD: 5/15 - 6/15

STARTING BALANCE ⟶ $ 2,312.70

DATE	DESCRIPTION	CHECK NUMBER	TRANSACTION AMOUNT	BALANCE
8/16	W/D	1056	$ 256.00	
8/20	DEPOSIT		$ 1,200.80	
8/22	W/D	Debit card	$ 234.81	
8/22	W/D	1058	$ 334.90	
8/23	W/D	Debit Card	$ 34.72	
8/25	W/D	1060	$ 145.78	
8/26	W/D	1059	$ 56.00	
8/27	DEPOSIT		$ 150.00	
9/1	W/D	1061	$ 230.00	

ENDING BALANCE ⟶ $2,368.29

NUMBER OR CODE	DATE	TRANSACTION DESCRIPTION	PAYMENT AMOUNT	✓	FEE	DEPOSIT AMOUNT	$ BALANCE 2,309.70
1056	8/15	Best Offer Inc.	256 00				- 256.00 / 2,053.70
1057	8/16	Dept. of Motor Vehicles	86 50				- 86.50 / 1,967.20
1058	8/16	AutoWorld	334 90				- 334.90 / 1,632.30
	8/18	Car Nation	234 81				- 234.81 / 1,397.49
	8/20	Deposit				1,200 80	+ 1,200.80 / 2,598.29
1059	8/21	Print Makers	56 00				- 56.00 / 2,542.29
1060	8/22	Book Bonanza	145 78				- 145.78 / 2,396.51
	8/23	Fast Freddy's Fast Food	34 72				- 34.72 / 2,361.79
	8/27	Deposit				150 00	+ 150.00 / 2,511.79
1061	8/30	Lincoln Savings Bank	230 00				- 230.00 / 2,281.79
1062	9/1	VOID					
1063	9/1	Pasta Pete's	32 50				- 32.50 / 2,249.29
	9/2	Deposit				300 00	+ 300.00 / 2,549.29

Checking Account Summary

Ending Balance from Statement	a.
Deposits Outstanding	+ b.
Total of Checks Outstanding	– c.
Revised statement balance	d.
Balance from Checkbook	e.

2-3 | Savings Accounts

Exercises

1. Gary deposits $3,700 in an account that pays 2.15% simple interest. He keeps the money in the account for three years, but doesn't make any deposits or withdrawals. How much interest will he receive after the three years?

2. How much simple interest is earned on $6,000 at an interest rate of 2.25% in $4\frac{1}{2}$ years?

3. How much principal would you have to deposit to earn $700 simple interest in $1\frac{1}{2}$ years at a rate of 2%.?

4. Jesse estimates that it will cost $300,000 to send his newborn son to a private college in 18 years. He currently has $65,000 to deposit in an account. What simple interest rate would he need so that $65,000 grows into $300,000 in 18 years? Round to the nearest percent.

5. Dillon has a bank account that pays 3.2% simple interest. His balance is $1,766. How long will it take for the amount in the account to grow to $2,000? Round to the nearest year.

6. How long will it take $5,000 to double in an account that pays 1.6% simple interest? Round to the nearest year.

7. How much simple interest would $1,500 earn in 11 months at an interest rate of 3.75%?

8. How much simple interest would $1,000 earn in 275 days at an interest rate of 4.21%? (There are 365 days in a year.)

9. Colin deposited $1,230 in an account that pays 2.19% simple interest for three years.

   a. What will the interest be for the three years?

   b. What will be the new balance after three years?

   c. How much interest did the account earn the first year, to the nearest cent?

   d. How much interest did the account earn the second year, to the nearest cent?

   e. How much interest did the account earn the third year, to the nearest cent?

10. Gerry deposited $1,230 in an account that pays 2.19% simple interest for one year.

    a. How much interest will he earn in one year?

    b. What will his balance be after one year?

    c. Gerry withdraws all of the principal and interest after the first year and deposits it into another one-year account at the same rate. What will his interest be for the second year?

    d. What will his balance be after two years?

    e. Compare the accounts of Gerry and Colin from Exercise 9. Who earned more interest the second year, Gerry or Colin? Explain.

11. Use the simple interest formula to find the missing entries in the following table. Round monetary amounts to the nearest cent, percents to the nearest hundredth of a percent, and time to the nearest month. Use 365 days = 1 year.

	Interest	Principal	Rate	Time
a.		$980	2.6%	1 yr
b.		$2,900	3.05%	15 mo
	$400	$3,500	4.5%	**c.**
	$400	**d.**	0.66%	4 years
	$400	$3,000	**e.**	3 yr
f.		$750,000	1.2%	100 days
	y dollars	p	2.11%	**g.**

12. How much simple interest would x dollars earn in 13 months at a rate of r percent?

13. How long would $100,000 take to double at a simple interest rate of 8%?

14. How long would $450 take to double at a simple interest rate of 100%?

15. What simple interest rate, to the nearest tenth, is needed for $15,000 to double in 8 years?

16. Arrange these fractions of a year in ascending order: 190 days, 5 months, 160 days, 7 months, 200 days.

17. Max has $17 in a fund he is creating to save for a bike. He adds $6 per week of his babysitting earnings to the fund. If his weekly fund balance is represented by an arithmetic sequence, find the 27th term.

2-4 Explore Compound Interest

Exercises

Round to the nearest cent where necessary.

1. How much interest would $2,000 earn in one year at the rate of 1.2%?

2. How much interest would $2,000 earn, compounded annually, in two years at the rate of 1.2%?

3. How much interest would $2,000 earn, with simple interest, in two years at the rate of 1.2%?

4. Compare your answers to Exercises 2 and 3. Explain why they differ.

5. How much would d dollars earn in one year at the rate of p percent compounded annually?

6. Margaret deposits $1,000 in a savings account that pays 1.4% interest compounded semiannually. What is her balance after one year?

7. How much interest does $5,300 earn at a rate of 2.8% interest compounded quarterly, in three months?

8. Mr. Guny deposits $4,900 in a savings account that pays 1.5% interest compounded quarterly.

   a. Find the first quarter's interest. b. Find the first quarter's balance.

   c. Find the second quarter's interest. d. Find the second quarter's balance.

   e. Find the third quarter's interest. f. Find the third quarter's balance.

   g. Find the fourth quarter's interest. h. Find the fourth quarter's balance.

   i. How much interest does the account earn in the first year?

9. Jonathan deposits $6,000 in a savings account that pays 2.1% interest compounded quarterly. What is his balance after one year?

10. How much interest would $1,000,000 earn at 2% compounded daily, in one day?

11. How much interest would y dollars earn in one day at a rate of 1.75% compounded daily?

12. Mrs. Huber opened a savings account on June 26 with a $1,300 deposit. The account pays 1.6% interest compounded daily. On June 27, she deposited $450 and on June 28 she withdrew $110. Complete the table based on Mrs. Huber's banking activity.

	June 26	June 27	June 28
Opening balance	a.	f.	k.
Deposit	b.	g.	—
Withdrawal	—	—	l.
Principal used to Compute Interest	c.	h.	m.
Interest	d.	i.	n.
Ending Balance	e.	j.	o.

13. Mr. Nolan has a bank account that compounds interest daily at a rate of 1.7%. On the morning of December 7, the principal is $2,644.08. That day he withdraws $550 to pay for a snow blower. Later that day he receives a $934 paycheck from his employer, and he deposits that in the bank. On December 8, he withdraws $300 to go holiday shopping. What is his balance at the end of the day on December 8?

14. Mrs. Platt has an account that pays p percent interest compounded daily. On April 27, she had an opening balance of b dollars. Also on April 27, she made a w dollars withdrawal and a d dollars deposit. Express her interest for April 27 algebraically.

15. This morning, Mrs. Rullan had a balance of 1,000 dollars in an account that pays 2.05% interest compounded weekly. Express her interest for the following week if she makes no deposits or withdrawals.

16. Kristin deposited $9,000 in an account that has an annual interest rate of 2.1% compounded monthly. How much interest will she earn at the end of one month?

17. How much would $25,000 earn in one hour at the rate of 5%, compounded hourly?

18. The Jules Server Scholarship Fund gives a graduation award of $250 to a graduating senior at North End High School. Currently the fund has a balance of $8,300 in an account that pays 2.2% interest compounded annually. Will the amount earned in annual interest be enough to pay for the award?

19. Kelly has d dollars in an account that pays 1.4% interest compounded weekly. Express her balance after one week algebraically.

Name _____ Date _____

2-5 | Compound Interest Formula

Exercises

Round to the nearest cent wherever necessary.

1. Mr. Mady opens a savings account with principal *P* dollars that pays 2.11% interest compounded quarterly. Express his ending balance after one year algebraically.

2. Jeff deposits $2,300 at 1.13% interest compounded weekly. What will be his ending balance after one year?

3. Nancy has $4,111 in an account that pays 1.07% interest compounded monthly. What is her ending balance after two years?

4. Mr. Weinstein has a savings account with a balance of $19,211.34. It pays 1.1% interest compounded daily. What is his ending balance after three years, if no other deposits or withdrawals are made? How much interest does he earn over the three years?

5. If you invested $10,000 at 3.8% compounded hourly for five years, what would be your ending balance?

6. Danielle has a CD at Crossland Bank. She invests $22,350 for four years at 1.55% interest, compounded monthly. What is her ending balance? How much interest did she make?

7. Ms. Santoro is opening a one-year CD for $16,000. The interest is compounded daily. She is told by the bank representative that the annual percentage rate (APR) is 1.8%. What is the annual percentage yield (APY) for this account?

8. Knob Hill Savings Bank offers a one-year CD at 1.88% interest compounded daily. What is the APY for this account? Round to the nearest hundredth of a percent.

9. Kings Park Bank is advertising a special 1.66% APR for CDs. Kevin takes out a one-year CD for $24,000. The interest is compounded daily. Find the APY for Kevin's account.

10. Imagine that you invest $100,000 in an account that pays 5.9% annual interest compounded monthly. What will your balance be at the end of 18 years?

11. Yurik invests $88,000 in a CD that is locked into a 1.75% interest rate compounded monthly, for seven years. How much will Yurik have in the account when the CD matures?

12. Stephanie has created a study tool to help her study compound interest. She writes the compound interest formula with letters different than the traditional representations.

$$X = M\left(1+\frac{Q}{K}\right)^{KB}$$

   a. If Q is increased, does the new balance increase or decrease? Explain your answer.

   b. If K is decreased, does the new balance increase or decrease? Explain.

   c. If B is increased, does the new balance increase or decrease? Explain.

   d. Is it possible that $M > X$? Explain.

   e. Using Stephanie's variable representation, express the amount of interest earned on the account.

13. Compare the simple interest for one year on a principal of 1 million dollars at an interest rate of 6.3% to compounding every second for the same principal and interest rate.

   a. How many seconds are in an hour?

   b. How many seconds are in a day?

   c. How many seconds are in a year?

   d. How much interest does $1,000,000 earn in one year at 6.3% interest, compounded every second?

   e. How much does the same $1,000,000 earn at 6.3% in one year, under simple interest?

   f. How much more interest did the compounded every second account earn when compared to the simple-interest account?

14. Britney invested $4,000 in a CD at TTYL Bank that pays 1.4% interest compounded monthly.

   a. How much will Britney have in her account at the end of one year?

   b. What is the APY for this account? Round to the nearest hundredth of a percent.

15. How much more would $5,000 earn in 10 years, compounded daily at 2%, when compared to the interest on $5,000 over 10 years, at 2% compounded semiannually?

2-6 | Continuous Compounding

Exercises

Round to the nearest cent wherever necessary.

1. Given the function $f(x) = \frac{1,234,999}{x}$, as the values of x increase toward infinity, what happens to the values of $f(x)$?

2. As the values of x increase toward infinity, what happens to the values of $g(x) = 3x - 19$?

3. Given the function, $h(x) = \frac{8x-3}{4x+5}$, as the values of x increase towards infinity, use a table to find out what happens to the values of $h(x)$.

4. If $f(x) = \frac{10}{x^2}$ use a table and your calculator to find $\lim_{x \to \infty} f(x)$.

5. Given the function $f(x) = 2^x$, find $\lim_{x \to \infty} f(x)$.

6. Given the function $f(x) = \left(\frac{1}{2}\right)^x$, use a table to compute $\lim_{x \to \infty} f(x)$.

7. If you deposit $1,000 at 100% simple interest, what will your ending balance be after one year?

In 8–12, you compare simple interest with daily compounding and continuous compounding.

8. If you deposit $10,000 at 1.85% simple interest, what would your ending balance be after three years?

9. If you deposit $10,000 at 1.85% interest, compounded daily, what would your ending balance be after three years?

10. If you deposit $10,000 at 1.85% interest, compounded continuously, what would your ending balance be after three years?

11. How much more did the account that was compounded continuously earn compared to the account compounded daily?

12. How much more did the account that was compounded daily earn compared to the simple-interest account?

13. Eric deposits $4,700 at 1.03% interest, compounded continuously for five years.

    a. What is his ending balance?

    b. How much interest did the account earn?

14. Write the verbal sentence that is the translation of $\lim\limits_{x \to \infty} f(x) = 3.66$.

15. Write the verbal sentence given below symbolically using limit notation.

    The limit of g(x), as x approaches zero, is fifteen.

16. Given the function $f(x) = \frac{2x-17}{x}$, use a table to find $\lim\limits_{x \to \infty} f(x)$.

17. Find the balance for each compounding period on $50,000 for $2\frac{1}{2}$ years at a rate of 1.3%.

    a. Annually   **b.** Semiannually

    c. Quarterly   **d.** Monthly

    e. Daily   **f.** Hourly

    g. Continuously

18. A private university has an endowment fund that currently has 49 million dollars in it. If it is invested in a one-year CD that pays 2% interest compounded continuously, how much interest will it earn?

19. Use a table of increasing values of x to find each of the following limits.

    a. $\lim\limits_{x \to \infty} f(x)$ if $f(x) = \frac{5x-2}{x+3}$ **b.** $\lim\limits_{x \to \infty} g(x)$ if $g(x) = \frac{12x+5}{4x+3}$

    c. $\lim\limits_{x \to \infty} f(x)$ if $f(x) = \frac{5x^3-100}{x^2}$ **d.** $\lim\limits_{x \to \infty} f(x)$ if $f(x) = \frac{7x^2-1}{x^3+2}$

20. Find the interest earned on a $14,000 balance for nine months at 1.1% interest compounded continuously.

21. Assume you had P dollars to invest in an account that paid 5% interest compounded continuously. How long would it take your money to double? (Hint: Try substituting different numbers of years into the continuous compounding formula). Round to the nearest year.

2-7 Future Value of Investments

Exercises

1. Vincent made a $2,000 deposit into an account on August 1 that yields 2% interest compounded annually. How much money will be in that account at the end of 5 years?

2. On December 31, Juan Carlos made a $7,000 deposit in an account that pays 0.9% interest compounded semi annually. How much will be in that account at the end of two years?

3. Liam was born on October 1, 2009. His grandparents put $20,000 into an account that yielded 3% interest compounded quarterly. When Liam turns 18, his grandparents will give him the money for a college education. How much will Liam get on his 18th birthday?

4. Colleen is 15 years from retiring. She opens an account at the Savings Bank. She plans to deposit $10,000 each year into the account, which pays 1.7% interest, compounded annually.

   a. How much will be in the account in 15 years?

   b. How much interest would be earned?

5. Anton opened an account at Bradley Bank by depositing $1,250. The account pays 2.325% interest compounded monthly. He deposits $1,250 every month for the next two years.

   a. How much will he have in the account at the end of the two-year period?

   b. Write the future value function. Let x represent each of the monthly interest periods.

   c. Graph the future value function.

   d. Using your graph, what will the approximate balance be after one year?

6. Sylvia wants to go on a cruise around the world in 5 years. If she puts $50 into an account each week that pays 2.25% interest compounded weekly, how much will she have at the end of the five-year period?

Name _____ Date _____

7. Fatima opened a savings account with $7,500. She decided to deposit that same amount semiannually. This account earns 1.975% interest compounded semiannually.

    a. What is the future value of the account after 10 years?

    b. Write the future value function. Let *x* represent the number of semiannual interest periods.

    c. Graph the future value function.

    d. Using your graph, what is the approximate amount in her account after 18 months?

8. Marina invests $200 every quarter into an account that pays 1.5% annual interest rate compounded quarterly. Adriana invests $180 in an account that pays 3% annual interest rate compounded quarterly.

    a. Determine the amount in Marina's account after 10 years.

    b. Determine the amount in Adriana's account after 10 years.

    c. Who had more money in the account after 10 years?

    d. Write the future value function for Marina's account.

    e. Write the future value function for Adriana's account.

    f. Graph Marina and Adriana's future value function on the same axes.

    g. Interpret the graph in the context of the two future value functions.

2-8 Present Value of Investments

Exercises

1. Complete the table to find the single deposit investment amounts.

Future Value	Rate	Time	Deposit (to nearest cent)
$200	2% compounded annually	2 yr	**a.**
$400	1.5% compounded semiannually	4 yr	**b.**
$5,000	1.1% compounded quarterly	8 yr	**c.**
$25,000	2.1% compounded monthly	64 mo	**d.**

2. Complete the table to find the periodic deposit investment amounts.

Future Value	Rate	Time	Deposit (to nearest cent)
$7,000	1.25% compounded annually	5 yr	**a.**
$9,500	2.6% compounded semiannually	8 yr	**b.**
$500,000	1.625% compounded quarterly	15 yr	**c.**
$1,000,000	2% compounded monthly	246 mo	**d.**

3. When his daughter Alisa was born, Mike began saving for her wedding. He wanted to have saved about $30,000 by the end of 20 years. How much should Mike deposit into an account that yields 3% interest compounded annually in order to have that amount? Round your answer to the nearest thousand dollars.

4. How long will it take for $5,000 to grow to $10,000 in an account that yields 1.2% interest compounded annually. Experiment with the formula in your calculator using different years or use logarithms.

5. Martina will be attending 4 years of undergraduate school and four more years of graduate school. She wants to have $200,000 in her savings account when she graduates in 8 years. How much must she deposit in an account now at a 2.6% interest rate that compounds monthly to meet her goal? Round your answer to the nearest dollar.

6. Kate wants to install an in ground pool in five years. She estimates the cost will be $50,000. How much should she deposit monthly into an account that pays 1.6% interest compounded monthly in order to have enough money to pay for the pool in 5 years? Round your answer to the nearest dollar.

7. Amber wants to have saved $300,000 by some point in the future. She set up a direct deposit account with a 1.75% APR compounded monthly, but she is unsure of how much to periodically deposit for varying lengths of time. Set up a present value function and graph that function to depict the present values for this situation from 12 months to 240 months.

8. Geri wants $30,000 at the end of five years in order to pay for new siding on her house. If her bank pays 2.2% interest compounded annually, how much does she have to deposit each year in order to have that amount?

9. Uncle Al wants to open an account for his nieces and nephews that he hopes will have $100,000 in it after 25 years. How much should he deposit now into an account that yields 1.75% interest compounded monthly so he can be assured of meeting that goal amount?

10. Althea will need $30,000 for her nursing school tuition in 18 months. She has a bank account that pays 2.45% interest compounded monthly. How much does she have to put in each month to have enough money for the tuition?

11. Art opened an account online that pays 1.8% interest compounded monthly. He has a goal of saving $20,000 by the end of four years. How much will he need to deposit each month?

12. Anthony wants to repay the loan his parents gave him in three years. How much does he need to deposit into an account semiannually that pays 1.25% interest twice a year in order to have $35,000 to repay the loan?

13. Lorna needs $40,000 for a down payment when she buys her boat in 4 years. How much does she need to deposit into an account that pays 1.15% interest compounded quarterly in order to meet her goal?

Graph the present value function for this situation.

14. How much should Sandy deposit each month into a 2.85% account, which compounds interest monthly, if she wants to save $85,000? Use a span from year 0 to year 10 in months.

Name _____   Date _____

2-9 The Term of a Single Deposit Account

Exercises

1. In each of the following compound interest equations with t representing the account term, determine the number of times the account is compounded per year and the interest rate percent.

   a. $314{,}961.92 = 280{,}000(1.04)^t$

   b. $4{,}050 = 1{,}800(1.0125)^{4t}$

   c. $2{,}142 = 350(1.006)^{2t}$

   d. $10{,}008 = 1{,}200(1.0036)^{12t}$

   e. $578.88 = 500(1.007)^{3t}$

2. Rewrite each of the compound interest equations in #2 as an exponential equation in the standard form $a = b^c$.

3. Solve for t in each of the following compound interest equations. Leave your answer in terms of a logarithm.

   a. $12{,}800 = 640(1.008)^{2t}$

   b. $32{,}500 = 5{,}000(1.04)^t$

   c. $9{,}800 = 1{,}000(1.0025)^{12t}$

   d. $18{,}500 = 500(1.00375)^{4t}$

   e. $39{,}000 = 30{,}000(1.006)^{3t}$

4. In each of the equations below, t represents the term of a savings account. Find the value of t to the nearest tenth of a year.

   a. $t = \dfrac{\log_{1.02}(2.875)}{12}$

   b. $t = \dfrac{\log_{1.12}(3.4)}{3}$

   c. $t = \dfrac{\log_{1.011}(100.15)}{2}$

   d. $t = \dfrac{\log_{1.025}(20.7)}{6}$

   e. $t = \dfrac{\log_{1.009}(8.125)}{12}$

5. In each of the following compound interest equations, the variable n represents the number of times per year that the interest is compounded. Use logarithms to write an expression for n. Evaluate the expression to the nearest integer.

    a. $6{,}720 = 6{,}400(1.00125)^{6n}$ **b.** $12{,}150 = 9{,}000(1.005)^{10n}$

    c. $762.5 = 625(1.008)^{4n}$ **d.** $232{,}200 = 180(1.051)^{12n}$

    e. $1{,}860 = 150(1.0625)^{3n}$

6. Shannon wants to start saving for her retirement. Her goal is to save $350,000. If she deposits $250,000 into an account that pays 2.04% interest compounded monthly, approximately how long will it take for her money to grow to the desired amount? Round your answer to the nearest tenth of a year.

7. Steve has $125,000 to invest in a savings account that pays 3.25% interest compounded quarterly. How many years will it take for the account to earn $15,000 in interest? Round your answer to the nearest tenth of a year.

8. Daisy deposited $600 into an account that compounds interest daily at a rate of 1.46%. At the end of a certain period of time, he had a balance in the account of $645.

    a. Write an expression for the account term t but do not evaluate it.

    b. Using the expression you determined in part **a** and the change-of-base formula with common logarithms, determine a value of the account term t.

    c. Using the expression you determined in part **a** and the change-of-base formula with natural logarithms, determine a value of the account term t. Round the term to the nearest year.

    d. What do you notice about the values of t found in parts **c** and **d**? Explain your reasoning for the results.

9. Jasper deposits $20,000 into an account that compounds interest continuously at a rate of 3.4%. To the nearest tenth of a year, how long will it take his money to grow to $30,500?

10. The time it takes for money to quadruple in an account where *r* is the interest rate expressed as a decimal compounded annually is given by the formula $t = \dfrac{\log 4}{\log(1+r)}$. Use the compound interest formula to derive this result.

11. Andy deposited $15,000 in an account that yields 2.8% interest compounded quarterly. How long will it take for his balance to increase by 25%?

Name _____ Date _____

2-10 The Term of a Systematic Account

Exercises

1. Use the Power Property of logarithms to determine the value. In some cases, there will be a numerical answer. In others the answer will be an algebraic expression.

   a. $\log(10^5)$

   b. $\log(a^2)$

   c. $\log_y 3^x$

   d. $\ln e^m$

   e. $\ln(a+b)^c$

2. Use the change of base property to write the given logarithm as a quotient of common logs. Do not evaluate.

   a. $\log_6 144$

   b. $\log_a(b-c)$

   c. $\log_7 t$

   d. $\log_{ab} 5$

   e. $\ln k$

3. Use the One-To-One Property and the Power Property to find the value of t to the nearest tenth in each of the following.

   a. $15.625 = (2.5)^t$

   b. $8^t = 26,2144$

   c. $5^{2t} = 9,765,625$

   d. $(3.5)^{2t+1} = 525.21875$

   e. $3^{\frac{t}{2}} + 10 = 6,571$

4. Use the compound interest formula $B = P(1+\frac{r}{n})^{nt}$ in each of the following to express t in terms of a logarithm by rewriting the exponential equation in logarithmic form. Simplify where possible but do not evaluate.

   a. $B = 800, P = 500, r = .02, n = 2$

   b. $B = 13,520, P = 5,200, r = .03, n = 6$

   c. $B = 750,000, P = 500,000, r = .036, n = 4$

Use the following situation for questions 5 and 6. Barbara has deposited money into a savings account at Center City Bank. The account pays 3% interest compounded monthly. How long will it take for $5,000 to grow to $5,600.

5. Use the steps below to find the value of t to the nearest year.

   a. Substitute the values in the compound interest formula.

   b. Simplify the value inside the parentheses.

   c. Divide both sides by the value of P. You should now have an exponential equation in standard form.

   d. Rewrite the exponential equation in an equivalent logarithmic form.

   e. Apply the change of base formula to change the logarithm into a quotient of two common logs.

   f. Find the value of the quotient to the nearest thousandth.

   g. Divide both sides by the coefficient of t. Round to the nearest tenth of a year.

6. Use the steps below to find the value of t to the nearest year.

   a. Substitute the values in the compound interest formula.

   b. Simplify the value inside the parentheses.

   c. Divide both sides by the value of P. You should now have an exponential equation in standard form.

   d. Apply the One-To-One Property using common logs.

   e. Simplify the side of the equation with the exponent by applying the Power Property.

   f. Solve for t. This will be a three-step process. Divide both sides by the logarithmic coefficient; divide both sides by the value of n; simplify and round to the nearest tenth of a year.

Questions 5 and 6 offered the steps for finding the term of a savings account using two different methods. Select either method to solve questions 7 and 8.

7. iPartner is an online bank that offers a locked-in interest rate of 3.6% compounded monthly. Rich makes an initial deposit of $10,000. How long does he have to keep the money in this account in order to have a balance of $12,000? Round to the nearest year.

8. Danka opened a savings account that pays 1.8% interest compounded continuously. Her initial deposit was $160. How long would she have to leave the money in the account for it to reach $250?

9. Bill want to make monthly deposits of $75 into a savings account that offers 2.7% interest compounded monthly. Use the future balance of a periodic investment formula to determine how long will it take for the account balance to reach $2000. Round to the nearest tenth of a year.

10. If Graziela makes quarterly deposits of $800 into an account that pays 1.8% interest quarterly, how long will it take for her principal to grow to $20,000? Use the future balance of a periodic investment formula to answer the question. Round to the nearest tenth of a year.

11. An alternative method for solution to problems similar to Exercises 9 and 10 would have been to use the present value formula from section 2-8 as shown here:

$$P = \frac{B \times \dfrac{r}{n}}{\left(1 + \dfrac{r}{n}\right)^{nt} - 1}$$

In a–h below, write the equations that result when you follow the steps to use this formula to solve exercise 10.

a. Let $B = 20{,}000$, $P = 800$, $r = 0.018$, and $n = 4$. Substitute these values into the present value formula.

b. Simplify wherever possible.

c. Eliminate the denominator. Multiply both sides of the equation by the expression in the denominator.

d. You will now try to isolate the variable t on one side of the equation. Divide both sides by 800.

e. Add 1 to both sides of the equation.

f. You now should have an exponential equation in standard form. Apply the One-To-One Property by taking the common log of both sides of the equation.

g. Apply the Power Property to remove the exponent.

h. Solve for t. Round your answer to the nearest tenth. Your result should match the answer in exercise 11.

12. In **a–h** below, write the equations that result when you follow the steps to use the systematic withdrawal formula, $P = W \dfrac{1-(1+\frac{r}{n})^{-nt}}{\frac{r}{n}}$ to determine how long it will take for a savings account to reach $0. The account was set up with an initial deposit of $8000. Interest is compounded monthly at 1.2% with a monthly withdrawal of $400.

a. Substitute $P = 8,000$, $W = 400$, $r = .012$, and $n = 12$ in the systematic withdrawal formula.

b. Simplify wherever possible.

c. Divide both sides by 400.

d. Multiply both sides by .001.

e. Subtract 1 from both sides.

f. Divide both sides by –1.

g. Take the log of both sides (One-To-One Property).

h. Apply the Power Property.

i. Divide both sides by log(1.001).

j. Divide both sides by –12.

k. Simplify.

13. Burt deposited $100,000 into an account that compounds interest semiannually at a rate of 2.66%. At the end of each 6-month period, a withdrawal of $8000 is made from the account. How long will it take until the account has a balance of $0? Round your answer to the nearest tenth of a year.

3-1 Introduction to Consumer Credit

Exercises

1. Monique purchases a $5,100 dining room set. She can't afford to pay cash, so she uses the installment plan, which requires an 18% down payment. How much is the down payment?

2. Joe wants to purchase an electric keyboard. The price of the keyboard at Macelli's, with tax, is $2,344. He can save $150 per month. How long will it take him to save for the keyboard?

3. Lisa purchases a professional racing bicycle that sells for $3,000, including tax. It requires a $200 down payment. The remainder, plus a finance charge, is paid back monthly over the next $2\frac{1}{2}$ years. The monthly payment is $111.75. What is the finance charge?

4. The price of a stove is s dollars. Pedro makes a 10% down payment for a two-year installment purchase. The monthly payment is m dollars. Express the finance charge algebraically.

5. Depot Headquarters has a new promotional payment plan. All purchases can be paid off on the installment plan with no interest, as long as the total is paid in full within 12 months. There is a $25 minimum monthly payment required. If the Koslow family buys a hot tub for $4,355, and they make only the minimum payment for 11 months, how much will they have to pay in the 12th month?

6. The White family purchases a new pool table on a no-interest-for-one-year plan. The cost is $2,665. There is a d dollars down payment. If they make a minimum monthly payment of m dollars until the last month, express their last month's payment algebraically.

7. Snow-House sells a $1,980 snow thrower on the installment plan. The installment agreement includes a 20% down payment and 12 monthly payments of $161 each.

   a. How much is the down payment?

   b. What is the total amount of the monthly payments?

   c. What is the total cost of the snow thrower on the installment plan?

   d. What is the finance charge?

8. Carey bought a $2,100 computer system on the installment plan. He made a $400 down payment, and he has to make monthly payments of $79.50 for the next two years. How much interest will he pay?

9. Mike bought a set of golf clubs that cost k dollars. He signed an installment agreement requiring a 5% down payment and monthly payments of g dollars for $1\frac{1}{2}$ years.

   a. Express his down payment algebraically.

   b. How many monthly payments must Mike make?

   c. Write expressions for the total amount of the monthly payments and the finance charge.

10. Mrs. Grudman bought a dishwasher at a special sale. The dishwasher regularly sold for $912. No down payment was required. Mrs. Grudman has to pay $160 for the next six months. What is the average amount she pays in interest each month?

11. The Hut sells a $2,445 entertainment system credenza on a six-month layaway plan.

    a. If the monthly payment is $440, what is the sum of the monthly payments?

    b. What is the fee charged for the layaway plan?

    c. Where is the credenza kept during the six months of the layaway plan?

12. Jessica has $70,000 in the bank and is earning 1.7% compounded monthly. She plans to purchase a used car, for which the down payment is $500 and the monthly payments are $280.

    a. Will her monthly interest cover the cost of the down payment? Explain.

    b. Will her monthly interest cover the cost of the monthly payment?

13. Joseph purchased a laptop that regularly sold for w dollars but was on sale at 10% off. He had to pay t dollars for sales tax. He bought it on the installment plan and had to pay 15% of the total cost with tax as a down payment. His monthly payments were m dollars per month for three years.

    a. Write expressions for the amount of the discount and the sale price.

    b. Write expressions for the total cost of the laptop, with tax, and the down payment.

    c. What was the total of all of the monthly payments? What was the total he paid for the widget on the installment plan?

    d. What was the finance charge?

3-2 | Loans

Exercises

Round to the nearest cent wherever necessary.

1. Refer to the table to find the monthly payments necessary to complete parts a–e.

   a. What is the monthly payment for a $3,200 five-year loan with an APR of 3%.

   b. Mia borrows $66,000 for four years at an APR of 4%. What is the monthly payment?

   c. What is the total amount of the monthly payments for a $6,100, two-year loan with an APR of 5%? Round to the nearest dollar.

Monthly Payment Per $1,000 of Loan				
Interest Rate (APR)	2-Year Loan	3-Year Loan	4-Year Loan	5-Year Loan
1%	$42.10	$28.21	$21.26	$17.09
2%	$42.54	$28.64	$21.70	$17.53
3%	$42.98	$29.08	$22.13	$17.97
4%	$43.42	$29.52	$22.58	$18.42
5%	$43.87	$29.97	$23.03	$18.87
6%	$44.32	$30.42	$23.49	$19.33
7%	$44.77	$30.88	$23.95	$19.80

   d. The total of monthly payments for a three-year loan is $22,317.12. The APR is 4%. How much money was originally borrowed?

   e. What is the finance charge for a $7,000, two-year loan with a 6% APR?

2. Ray borrows b dollars over a $2\frac{1}{2}$-year period. The monthly payment is m dollars. Express his finance charge algebraically.

3. Cecilia bought a new car. The total amount she needs to borrow is $29,541. She plans to take out a four-year loan at an APR of 6.3%. What is the monthly payment?

4. Claire needs to borrow $12,000 from a local bank. She compares the monthly payments for a 5.1% loan for three different periods of time. What is the monthly payment for a one-year loan? A two-year loan? A five-year loan?

5. The Star Pawnshop will lend up to 45% of the value of a borrower's collateral. Ryan wants to use $4,000 worth of jewelry as collateral for a loan. What is the maximum amount that he could borrow from Star?

6. Solomon is taking out a loan of x dollars for y years, which has a monthly payment of m dollars. Express the finance charge for this loan algebraically.

7. Jeanne has a $14,800, $3\frac{1}{2}$-year loan with a high APR of 8.56% due to her less-than-average credit rating.

 a. What is the monthly payment for this loan?

 b. If she changes the loan to a three-year loan, what is the monthly payment?

 c. What is the difference in the monthly payments for the two loans?

 d. Which loan has the higher finance charge? What is the difference in the finance charge for these two loans?

 e. Do you feel that it is worth paying the higher monthly payment to have the loan finish six months earlier?

8. Liz found an error in the monthly payment her bank charged her for a four-year, $19,500 loan. She took the loan out at an APR of 5%. Her bank was charging her $459.07 per month.

 a. What is the correct monthly payment?

 b. Liz noticed the error just before making the last payment. The bank told her that they would credit all of the overpayments and adjust her last month's payment accordingly. What should her last month's payment be after the adjustment? Explain.

9. The Bartolotti family took out a loan to have a garage built next to their house. The 10-year, 10.4% loan was for $56,188. The monthly payment was $475, but the promissory note stated that there was a balloon payment at the end.

 a. How many monthly payments do the Bartolotti's have to make?

 b. What is the sum of all but the last monthly payment?

 c. If the finance charge is $34,415.60, what must the total of all of the monthly payments be?

 d. What is the amount of the balloon payment for the final month of this loan?

10. Christina is a police officer, so she can use the Police and Fire Credit Union. The credit union will lend her $11,000 for three years at 4.05% APR. The same loan at her savings bank has an APR of 6.82%.

 a. How much would Christina save on the monthly payment if she takes the loan from the credit union?

 b. How much would she save in finance charges by taking the loan from the credit union?

3-3 Student Loans

Use the following situation to answer questions 1–5.

Marlie will be starting college next month. She was approved for a 10-year, Federal Unsubsidized student loan in the amount of $18,800 at 4.29%. She knows she has the option of beginning repayment of the loan in 4.5 years. She also knows that during this non-payment time, interest will accrue at 4.29%.

1. How much interest will Marlie accrue during the 4.5-year non-payment period?

2. Marlie has to decide whether she can afford to make interest-only payments for the first 4.5 years or defer all payments for that period of time. If she decides to make no payments during the 4.5 years, the interest will be capitalized at the end of that period. Suppose Marlie decides to defer the payments.

    a. What will be the new principal when she begins making loan payments?

    b. How much interest will she pay over the life of the loan?

3. Suppose Marlie only paid the interest during her 4 years in school and the six-month grace period. What will she now pay in interest over the term of the loan?

4. Marlie made her last monthly interest-only payment on December 1. Her next payment is due on January 1. What will be the amount of that interest-only payment?

5. Suppose that Marlie had decided to apply for a private loan rather than a federal loan. She has been offered a private loan for 10 years with an APR of 7.8%.

    a. Determine her monthly payment.

    b. What is the total amount she will pay back?

    c. What is the total interest amount?

6. Jim's parents paid for the first three years of his college costs. When he was a college senior, he was approved for an unsubsidized loan in the amount of $15,200 at a 4.29% interest rate for 10 years.

    a. If he chooses to make interest-only payments until the monthly loan payments are due, for how long will he be making interest only payments?

    b. What is the total amount of his interest-only payments?

    c. If he begins the loan repayment with no interest capitalization because he already paid the interest when he was in school and during the six-month grace period, how much will he have paid in interest for this loan by the end of the 10-year loan period?

7. Barb is a freshman attending a 4-year college. She has been approved for a $12000 subsidized federal loan at 4.29% for 10 years. How much will the U.S. Department of Education pick up in interest costs during her 4.5-year non-payment period?

Use the following situation to answer questions 8–12.

Phil has been accepted into a 2-year Radiology Technician Program at a career school. He has been awarded a $9000 unsubsidized 10-year federal loan at 4.29%. He knows he has the option of beginning repayment of the loan in 2.5 years. He also knows that during this non-payment time, interest will accrue at 4.29%.

8. How much interest will Phil accrue during the 2.5-year non-payment period?

9. If Phil decides to make no payments during the 2.5 years, the interest will be capitalized at the end of that period. What will be the new principal when he begins making loan payments?

10. Suppose Phil only paid the interest during his 2 years in school and the six-month grace period. What will he pay in interest over the term of his loan?

11. Phil made his last monthly interest-only payment on April 12. His next payment is due on May. What will be the amount of that interest-only payment?

12. Suppose that Phil had decided to take out a private loan for $9,000 where loan payments start as soon as the loan amount is deposited in his student account and continue for 10 years. The interest rate is 8.1%.

    a. Determine his monthly payment.   b. What is the total amount he will pay back?

    c. What is the total interest amount?

3-4 Loan Calculations and Regression

Exercises

1. What is the monthly payment for a 10-year, $20,000 loan at 4.625% APR? What is the total interest paid on this loan?

2. Max is taking out a 5.1% loan in order to purchase a $17,000 car. The length of the loan is five years. How much will he pay in interest?

3. Merissa wants to borrow $12,000 to purchase a used boat. After looking at her monthly budget, she realizes that all she can afford to pay per month is $250. The bank is offering a 6.1% loan. What should the length of her loan be so that she can keep within her budget? Round to the nearest year.

4. What is the total interest on a 15-year, 4.98% loan with a principal of $40,000?

5. Ansel wants to borrow $10,000 from the Hampton County Bank. They offered him a 6-year loan with an APR of 6.35%. How much will he pay in interest over the life of the loan?

6. Tom and Kathy want to borrow $35,000 in order to build an addition to their home. Their bank will lend them the money for 12 years at an interest rate of $5\frac{3}{8}$%. How much will they pay in interest to the bank over the life of the loan?

Use the Yearly Payment Schedule to answer Exercises 7–10.

Year	Principal Paid	Interest Paid	Loan Balance	Year	Principal Paid	Interest Paid	Loan Balance
							$76,000.00
2016	$3,702.31	$3,158.45	$72,297.69	2024	$5,198.46	$1,662.30	$36,279.09
2017	$3,862.78	$2,997.98	$68,434.91	2025	$5,423.74	$1,437.02	$30,855.35
2018	$4,030.18	$2,830.58	$64,404.73	2026	$5,658.80	$1,201.96	$25,196.55
2019	$4,204.85	$2,655.91	$60,199.88	2027	$5,904.04	$956.72	$19,292.51
2020	$4,387.07	$2,473.69	$55,812.81	2028	$6,159.90	$700.86	$13,132.61
2021	$4,577.18	$2,283.58	$51,235.63	2029	$6,426.88	$433.88	$6,705.73
2022	$4,775.56	$2,085.20	$46,460.07	2030	$6,705.73	$157.40	$0.00
2023	$4,982.52	$1,878.24	$41,477.55				

7. What is the loan amount?

8. What is the length of the loan?

9. What is the monthly payment?

10. What is the total interest over the loan's life?

11. Neville is considering taking out a $9,000 loan. He went to two lending institutions. Sunset Park Company offered him a 10-year loan with an interest rate of 5.2%. Carroll Gardens Bank offered him an 8-year loan with an interest rate of 6.6%. Which loan will have the lowest interest over its lifetime?

12. JFK Federal Bank offers a $50,000 loan at an interest rate of 4.875% that can be paid back over 3 to 15 years.

    a. Write the monthly payment formula for this loan situation. Let t represent the number of years from 3 to 15 inclusive.

    b. Write the total interest formula for this loan situation. Let t represent the number of years from 3 to 15 inclusive.

Use the table of decreasing loan balances for a $230,000 loan at 5.5% for 20 years to answer questions 13–15.

13. Write a linear regression equation that models the data with numbers rounded to the nearest tenth.

14. Write a quadratic regression equation that models the data with numbers rounded to the nearest tenth.

15. Write a cubic regression equation that models the data with numbers rounded to the nearest tenth.

	Loan Balance
0	$230,000.00
1	$223,502.14
2	$216,637.75
3	$209,386.16
4	$201,725.52
5	$193,632.76
6	$185,083.51
7	$176,052.02
8	$166,511.07
9	$156,431.94
10	$145,784.26
11	$134,535.97
12	$122,653.20
13	$110,100.15
14	$96,839.02
15	$82,829.83
16	$68,030.43
17	$52,396.21
18	$35,880.12
19	$18,432.38
20	$0.00

3-5 | Credit Cards

Exercises

Round to the nearest cent wherever necessary.

1. If the APR on a credit card is 22.2%, what is the monthly interest rate?

2. If the monthly interest rate on a credit card is p percent, express the APR algebraically.

3. The average daily balance for Dave's last credit card statement was $1,213.44, and he had to pay a finance charge. The APR is 20.4%. What is the monthly interest rate? What is the finance charge for the month?

4. Mr. Reis had these daily balances on his credit card for his last billing period. He did not pay the card in full the previous month, so he will have to pay a finance charge. The APR is 19.8%.

    six days @ $341.22   ten days @ $987.45
    three days @ $2,122.33   eleven days @ $2,310.10

    a. What is the average daily balance?

    b. What is the finance charge?

5. Mrs. Fagin's daily balances for the past billing period are given below.
    For five days she owed $233.49.   For three days she owed $651.11.
    For nine days she owed $991.08.   For seven days she owed $770.00.
    For seven days she owed $778.25.

    Find Mrs. Fagin's average daily balance.

6. Mike Bauer had a daily balance of x dollars for d days, y dollars for 9 days, r dollars for 4 days, and m dollars for 5 days. Express his average daily balance algebraically.

7. Mrs. Cykman's credit card was stolen, and she did not realize it for several days. The thief charged a $440 watch while using it. According to the Truth-in-Lending Act, at most how much of this is Mrs. Cykman responsible for paying?

8. Mr. Kramden's credit card was lost on a vacation. He immediately reported it missing. The person who found it days later used it and charged c dollars worth of merchandise on the card, where $c > \$50$. How much of the c dollars is Mr. Kramden responsible for paying?

9. The average daily balance for Pete's credit card last month was a dollars. The finance charge was f dollars. Express the APR algebraically.

Name _____   Date _____

10. Brett and Andy applied for the same credit card from the same bank. The bank checked both of their FICO scores. Brett had an excellent credit rating, and Andy had a poor credit rating.

   a. Brett was given a card with an APR of 12.6%. What was his monthly percentage rate?

   b. Andy was given a card with an APR of 16.2%. What was his monthly percentage rate?

   c. If each of them had an average daily balance of $7,980, and had to pay a finance charge for that month, how much more would Andy pay than Brett?

11. A set of daily balances for one billing cycle are expressed algebraically below.

   w days @ r dollars   5 days @ x dollars   n days @ q dollars   p days @ $765

   If the APR is 21.6%, express the billing cycle's finance charge algebraically.

12. Mrs. Imperiale's credit card has an APR of 13.2%. She does not ever pay her balance off in full, so she always pays a finance charge. Her next billing cycle starts today. The billing period is 31 days long. She is planning to purchase $7,400 worth of new kitchen cabinets this billing cycle. She will use her tax refund to pay off her entire bill next month. If she purchases the kitchen cabinets on the last day of the billing cycle instead of the first day, how much would she save in finance charges? Round to the nearest ten dollars.

13. Pat's ending balance on his debit card last month was $233.55. This month he had $542 worth of purchases and $710 worth of deposits. What is his ending balance for this month?

14. Tomika's credit rating was lowered, and the credit card company raised her APR from 18% to 25.2%.

   a. If her average daily balance this month is $8,237, what is the increase in this month's finance charge due to the higher APR?

   b. If this amount is typical of Tomika's average daily balance all year, how much would the rise in interest rate cost her in a typical year? Round to the nearest ten dollars.

15. Linda and Rob charged a $67.44 restaurant bill on their credit card. They gave the card to the waitress, who accidentally transposed two digits and charged them $76.44. They did not notice this until they received their statement later that month. Their card has an 18% APR.

   a. How much were Linda and Rob overcharged?

   b. They plan to pay their monthly statement amount in full, but they need to deduct the amount they were overcharged, plus the finance charge that was based on the incorrect amount. If the overcharged amount was on their statement for 18 of the 31-day billing cycle, how much should they deduct from this monthly statement, including the amount they were overcharged?

3-6 Credit Card Statement

Exercises

1. The summary portion of Manny Ramira's credit card statement is shown. Determine the new balance amount.

SUMMARY	Previous Balance	Payments / Credits	Transactions	Late Charge	Finance Charge	New Balance	Minimum Payment
	1,237.56	$1,200.00	$2,560.67	$0.00	$9.56		

2. Lizzy has a credit line of $9,000 on her credit card. Her summary is shown. What is her available credit balance?

SUMMARY	Previous Balance	Payments / Credits	Transactions	Late Charge	Finance Charge	New Balance	Minimum Payment
	$6,500.56	$5,200.00	$978.45	$20.00	$12.88		

3. Rich had a previous balance of x dollars and made an on-time credit card payment of y dollars where $y < x$. He has a credit line of 10,000 dollars and will have to pay $15.50 in finance charges. Rich made purchases totaling $1,300.30. Write an algebraic expression that represents his current available credit.

4. Determine the error that was made using the following summary statement.

SUMMARY	Previous Balance	Payments / Credits	Transactions	Late Charge	Finance Charge	New Balance	Minimum Payment
	$350.90	$200.00	$200.00	$0.00	$8.68	$759.58	

5. Marianne has a credit card with a line of credit at $15,000. She made the following purchases: $1,374.90, $266.21, 39.46, and $903.01. What is Marianne's available credit?

6. Luke has a credit line of $8,500 on his credit card. He had a previous balance of $4,236.87 and made a $3,200.00 payment. The total of his purchases is $989.42. What is Luke's available credit?

7. The APR on Ramona's credit card is currently 24.6%. What is the monthly periodic rate?

8. Sheila's monthly periodic rate is 2.41%. What is her APR?

9. Examine the summary section of a monthly credit card statement. Calculate the new balance.

SUMMARY	Previous Balance	Payments / Credits	Transactions	Late Charge	Finance Charge	New Balance	Minimum Payment
	$876.34	$800.00	$1,009.56	$30.00	$29.67		$18.00

10. Jack set up a spreadsheet to model his credit card statement. The summary statement portion of the spreadsheet is shown. Write the formula for available credit that would be entered in cell J32.

	D	E	F	G	H	I	J
	Previous Balance	**Payments**	**New Purchases**	**Late Charge**	**Finance Charges**	**Credit Line**	**Available Credit**
31							
32							

11. Use the credit card statement to answer the questions below.

Liam DeWitt						6915 Maple Creek Dr. West Chester, OH

ACCOUNT INFORMATION						
Account Number	4-10700000		Billing Date	13 Sept	**Payment Due**	30 Sept

TRANSACTIONS		DEBITS / CREDITS (–)
22 Aug	Propane Home Heat	$250.50
23 Aug	TJ Marsha's Department Store	$87.60
25 Aug	Brighton University	$1,300.00
1 Sept	Middle Island Auto Parts	$470.63
2 Sept	Payment	– $2,000.00
3 Sept	Al's Mobal Gas Station	$34.76
5 Sept	Stop, Shop and Go	$102.71
10 Sept	Federal Express	$45.90
12 Sept	Computer Depot	$848.60

SUMMARY	Previous Balance	Payments / Credits	Transactions	Late Charge	Finance Charge	New Balance	Minimum Payment
	$3,240.50			$0.00			$50.00

Total Credit Line	$ 5,000.00	Average Daily Balance	# Days in Billing Cycle	APR	Monthly Periodic Rate
Total Available Credit	$ 5,000.00				
Credit Line for Cash	$ 4,000.00				
Available Credit for Cash	$ 4,000.00		30	19.8%	

a. How many purchases (debits) were made during the billing cycle?

b. What is the sum of all purchases (debits) made during the billing cycle?

c. When is the payment for this statement due?

d. What is the minimum amount that can be paid?

e. How many days are in the billing cycle?

f. What is the previous balance?

Name_____ Date _____

3-7 Average Daily Balance

Exercises

Use Liam DeWitt's Flash Card statement and the blank credit calendar for Exercises 1–4.

Liam DeWitt					6915 Maple Creek Dr. West Chester, OH	
ACCOUNT INFORMATION						
Account Number	4-10700000		Billing Date	13 Sept	**Payment Due**	30 Sept
TRANSACTIONS					DEBITS / CREDITS (−)	
22 Aug	Propane Home Heat				$250.50	
23 Aug	TJ Marsha's Department Store				$87.60	
25 Aug	Brighton University				$1,300.00	
1 Sept	Middle Island Auto Parts				$470.63	
2 Sept	Payment				− $2,000.00	
3 Sept	Al's Mobal Gas Station				$34.76	
5 Sept	Stop, Shop and Go				$102.71	
10 Sept	Federal Express				$45.90	
12 Sept	Computer Depot				$848.60	

SUMMARY	Previous Balance	Payments / Credits	Transactions	Late Charge	Finance Charge	New Balance	Minimum Payment
	$3,240.50			$0.00			$30.00

Total Credit Line	$ 5.000.00	Average Daily Balance	# Days in Billing Cycle	APR	Monthly Periodic Rate
Total Available Credit	$ 5,000.00				
Credit Line for Cash	$ 4,000.00				
Available Credit for Cash	$ 4,000.00		30	19.8%	

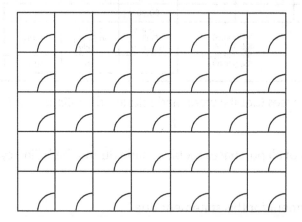

1. What is Liam's average daily balance?

2. What is Liam's monthly periodic rate?

3. What is Liam's finance charge?

4. What is Liam's new balance?

5. What is Liam's available credit?

1. What is Liam's average daily balance?

2. What is Liam's monthly periodic rate?

3. What is Liam's finance charge?

4. What is Liam's new balance?

5. What is Liam's available credit?

Name _____ Date _____

Use Shannon Houston's credit card statement and the blank calendar for Exercises 6–11.

Shannon Houston		720 Timber Trail Dr Indianapolis, IN

ACCOUNT INFORMATION		
Account Number 16677289-02	Billing Date 6 Apr	**Payment Due** 30 Apr

TRANSACTIONS		DEBITS / CREDITS ()
9 Mar	Gingham Pastry Shop	$27.68
11 Mar	Corner Clothes	$127.35
16 Mar	Le Petite Menu	$87.40
22 Mar	Payment	– $190.60
26 Mar	Dutchess Pharmacy	57.30
28 Mar	Sparrow Jewelers	$325.90
4 Apr	Elder's Antiques	$870.21

SUMMARY	Previous Balance	Payments / Credits	Transactions	Late Charge	Finance Charge	New Balance	Minimum Payment
	$560.30			$0.00			$25.00

Total Credit Line $ 5.000.00 Total Available Credit Credit Line for Cash $ 4,000.00 Available Credit for Cash $ 4,000.00	Average Daily Balance	# Days in Billing Cycle	APR	Monthly Periodic Rate
		30	15.6%	

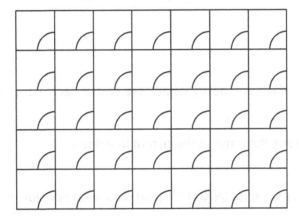

6. What amount should be in the box for "Payment/Credits"?

7. What amount should be in the box for "Transactions"?

8. What is Shannon's average daily balance?

9. What is Shannon's finance charge?

10. What is Shannon's new balance?

11. What is Shannon's available credit?

4-1 Classified Ads

Exercises

1. Enrique plans to sell his car and places a 6-line ad. His paper charges $42 for the first two lines and $6.75 per extra line, to run the ad for one week. What will Enrique's ad cost to run for three weeks?

2. The following piecewise function gives the cost, $c(x)$, of a classified ad in a car magazine.

$$c(x) = \begin{cases} 35.50 & \text{when } x \le 4 \\ 35.50 + 5.25(x-4) & \text{when } x > 4 \end{cases}$$

   a. Graph the function.

   b. If x is the number of lines in the ad, what is the cost of each extra line?

   c. Is the cost of one line the same as the cost of four lines?

3. Griffith purchased a used car for $9,400. He paid 6.5% sales tax. How much tax did he pay?

4. Ms. Boyrer is writing a program to compute ad costs. She needs to enter an algebraic representation of the costs of a local paper's ad. The charge is $32.25 for up to three lines for a classified ad. Each additional line costs $6. Express the cost of an ad $f(x)$ with x lines as a function of x algebraically.

5. *The Fort Salonga News* charges $29.50 for a classified ad that is four or fewer lines long. Each line above four lines costs an additional $5.25. Express the cost of an ad algebraically as a piecewise function.

6. Roxanne set up the following split function, which represents the cost of an auto classified ad from her hometown newspaper.

$$f(x) = \begin{cases} 31.50 & \text{when } x \le 5 \\ 31.50 + 5.50(x-5) & \text{when } x > 5 \end{cases}$$

If x is the number of lines in the ad, express the price $c(x)$ of a classified ad from this paper in words.

7. Dr. Mandel purchased a used car for $11,325. Her state charges 8% tax for the car, $53 for license plates, and $40 for a state safety and emissions inspection. How much does she need to pay for these extra charges, not including the price of the car?

8. Leeanne plans to sell her car and places an x-line ad. The newspaper charges p dollars for the first k lines and e dollars per extra line, to run the ad for a week.

   a. When $x > k$, write an algebraic expression for the cost of running the ad for a week.

   b. When $x < k$, write an algebraic expression for the cost of running the ad for two weeks.

9. A local *Pennysaver* paper charges f dollars weekly for a five-line classified ad. Each additional line costs a dollars. Express algebraically the cost of a four-line ad that runs for a year.

10. a. Graph the piecewise function: $f(x) = \begin{cases} 22.50 & \text{when } x \le 6 \\ 22.50 + 5.75(x-6) & \text{when } x > 6 \end{cases}$

   b. What are the coordinates of the cusp?

   c. What is the slope of the graph where $x > 6$?

   d. What is the slope of the graph where $x < 6$?

11. Mr. Ciangiola placed this ad in the *Collector Car Digest*:

> 2014 Chevrolet HHR SUV. Orange, 4 cyl.
> automatic, leather, chrome wheels, wood
> trim, running boards, PS, PB, AM/FM/CD.
> Mint! $18,500. 555-7331.

a. If the newspaper charges $45 for the first four lines and $7 for each extra line, how much will this ad cost?

b. Sue buys the car for 5% less than the advertised price. How much does she pay?

c. Sue must pay her state 4% sales tax on the sale. How much must she pay in sales tax?

12. Express the classified ad rate, $36 for the first four lines and $4.25 for each additional line, as a piecewise function. Use a "Let" statement to identify what x and y represent.

13. The following piecewise function represents the cost of an x-line classified ad from the *Rhinebeck Register*.

$$f(x) = \begin{cases} D & \text{when } x \le w \\ D + K(x - w) & \text{when } x > w \end{cases}$$

a. What is the cost of a p-line ad, if $p < w$?

b. What is the cost of a b-line ad, if $b > w$?

c. Express algebraically the total cost, with 6% sales tax, of a w-line ad.

4-2   Automobile Transactions

Exercises

1. The following automobile prices are listed in descending order: *a, b, c, d, x, y,* and *w*. Express the difference between the median and the mean of these prices algebraically.

2. A local charity wants to purchase a classic 1956 Thunderbird for use as a prize in a fundraiser. They find the following eight prices in the paper.

$48,000	$57,000	$31,000	$58,999
$61,200	$59,000	$97,500	$42,500

   a. What is the best measure of central tendency to use to get a reasonable estimate for the cost of the car? Explain.

   b. What is the range?

3. Given is the list of prices for a set of used original hubcaps for a 1957 Chevrolet. They vary depending on the condition. Find the following statistics for the hubcap prices.

   $120 $50 $320 $220 $310 $100 $260 $300 $155 $125
   $600 $250 $200 $200 $125

   a. mean, to the nearest dollar

   b. median

   c. mode

   d. four quartiles

   e. range

   f. interquartile range

   g. boundary for the lower outliers; any lower outliers

   h. boundary for the upper outliers; any upper outliers

Name _____ Date _____

4. The data below gives the MPG ratings for cars owned by 15 Placid High School seniors. Find the following statistics about the MPG ratings.

15.9, 17.8, 21.6, 25.2, 31.1, 29, 28.6, 32, 34, 14, 19.8, 19.5, 20.1, 27.7, 25.5

a. Mean

b. Median

c. median of the lowest seven scores

d. lower quartile, Q_1

e. median of the highest seven scores

f. upper quartile, Q_3

g. interquartile range

h. range

i. boundary for the upper outliers

j. boundary for the lower outliers

k. How many outliers are in this data set?

5. The following scores are written in ascending order: $a, b, c, d, e, f, g, h,$ and i.

a. What measure of central tendency does score e represent?

b. What measure of central tendency is represented by $\frac{a+b+c+d+e+f+g+h+i}{9}$?

c. Which quartile is represented by $\frac{b+c}{2}$?

6. The boxplot summarizes information about the numbers of hours worked in December for 220 seniors at Tomah High School.

a. What is the range? What is the interquartile range?

b. What percent of the students worked 68 or more hours?

c. How many students worked 31 hours or less?

d. Does the boxplot give the median of the distribution? What is the median?

7. Jerry is looking to purchase a set of used chrome wheels for his SUV. He found 23 ads for the wheels he wants online and in the classified ads of his local newspaper and arranged the prices in ascending order, which is given below.

$350	$350	$350	$420	$450	$450	$500	$500	$500	$500
$600	$700	$725	$725	$725	$725	$725	$775	$775	$800
$825	$825	$850							

a. Make a frequency table to display the data.

b. Find the mean.

c. Draw a box-and-whisker plot for the data.

8. *Collector Car Magazine* has a listing for many Chevrolet Nomads.

Price	Frequency
$29,000	2
$34,000	1
$35,000	1
$42,900	1
$48,000	5
$51,000	3
$56,000	1
$59,000	4

a. Find the total frequency.

b. Find the range.

c. Find the mean to the nearest cent.

d. Draw a box-and-whisker plot for the data.

9. Use the modified boxplot to determine if Statements a – g are True or False. When the statement is false, explain.

a. The range is $r - y$.

b. 25% of the scores are at or below y.

c. The interquartile range is $u - z$.

d. The median is w.

e. The boundary for lower outliers is r.

f. The boundary for upper outliers is y.

10. The side-by-side boxplots for distributions A and B were drawn on the same axes.

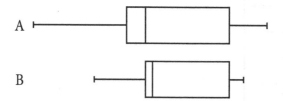

a. Which distribution has the greater range?

b. Which distribution has the lower first quartile?

c. Which distribution has the smallest interquartile range?

d. What percent of the scores in distribution A is above distribution B's maximum score?

e. Which distribution has scores that are the most varied?

f. What percent of scores in distribution A are less than distribution B's first quartile?

4-3 Automobile Insurance

Exercises

1. Mr. Cousins has 100/300 bodily injury insurance. He was in an auto accident caused by his negligence. Five people were injured in the accident. They sued in court and were awarded money. One person was awarded $150,000, and each of the other two was awarded $95,000. How much will the insurance company pay for these lawsuits?

2. Ronaldo has 50/250 BI liability insurance. He loses control of his car and injures 18 children in a Little League game, and each child is awarded $20,000 as a result of a lawsuit. How much will the insurance company pay in total for this lawsuit? How much will Ronaldo be personally responsible for?

3. Cai's annual premium is p dollars. If she pays her premium semiannually, there is a 1% surcharge on each payment. Write an expression for the amount of her semiannual payment.

4. Jake has $25,000 worth of property damage insurance and $1,000-deductible collision insurance. He caused an accident that damaged a $2,000 sign, and he also did $2,400 worth of damage to another car. His car had $2,980 worth of damage done.

    a. How much will the insurance company pay under Jake's property damage insurance?

    b. How much will the insurance company pay under Jake's collision insurance?

    c. How much of the damage must Jake pay for?

5. Allen Siegell has a personal injury protection policy that covers each person in, on, around, or under his car for medical expenses up to $50,000. He is involved in an accident and five people in his car are hurt. One person has $3,000 of medical expenses, three people each have $500 worth of medical expenses, and Allen himself has medical expenses totaling $62,000. How much money must the insurance company pay out for these five people?

6. The Chow family just bought a second car. The annual premium would have been a dollars to insure the car, but they are entitled to a 12% discount since they have another car insured by the company.

    a. Express their annual premium after the discount algebraically.

    b. If they pay their premium quarterly, and have to pay a quarterly b dollars surcharge for this arrangement, express their quarterly payment algebraically.

---

7. Mrs. Lennon has 100/275/50 liability insurance and $50,000 PIP insurance. During an ice storm, she hits a fence and bounces into a storefront with 11 people inside. Some are hurt and sue her. A passenger in Mrs. Lennon's car is also hurt.

   a. The storefront will cost $24,000 to replace. There was $1,450 worth of damage to the fence. What insurance will cover this, and how much will the company pay?

   b. A professional soccer player was in the store, and due to the injuries, he can never play soccer again. He sues for $3,000,000 and is awarded that money in court. What type of insurance covers this, and how much will the insurance company pay?

   c. The passenger in the car had medical bills totaling $20,000. What type of insurance covers this, and how much will the insurance company pay?

   d. The 11 people in the store are hurt and each requires $12,000 or less for medical attention. Will the company pay for all of these injuries?

8. In 2007, Roslyn High School instituted a safe driver course for all students who have licenses. They want to statistically analyze if the course is working. The side-by-side box-and-whisker plots give the annual number of car accidents involving Roslyn students for those two 10-year periods.

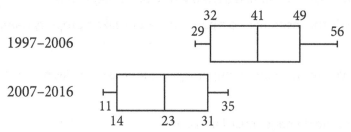

   a. What is the median number of annual accidents for the years 1997–2006? The years 2007–2016?

   b. What is the range of the annual accident figures for the years 1997–2006? The years 2007–2016?

   c. What do the side-by-side boxplots tell about the safe driver program that Roslyn High School instituted? Explain.

   d. John claims that 75% of the data for the years 2007–2016 are less than the first quartile for the years 1997–2006. Is he correct? Explain.

9. Manuel has x dollar-deductible collision insurance. His car is involved in an accident, and has w dollars worth of damage to it, where $x > w$. How much must the insurance company pay him for the damages?

4-4 Probability—The Basis of Insurance

Exercises

1. The distribution of ages of drivers at the Darcy Insurance Agency is normally distributed with mean 48 and standard deviation 10. As part of an advertising campaign, a driver is going to be selected at random to receive free car insurance for a year. What is the probability that the randomly selected person will be less than 30 years old?

2. The ratio of male drivers to female drivers with parking passes at Plandome High School is 5:3. If there are 64 students with parking passes, how many are female?

3. The following two-way table shows student lunch preferences for underclassmen at Minisink High School. Express your answers in fraction form.

	Freshman (F)	Sophomore (S)	Junior (J)	Total
Buy Lunch In School (B)	46	25	49	120
Bring Own Lunch (L)	36	65	44	145
Total	82	90	93	265

   a. Find the probability that a randomly selected person from this group brings their own lunch.

   b. What is the probability that a randomly selected person from this group is a freshman who brings their own lunch?

   c. Find the probability that a randomly selected person from this group is a junior given that they buy lunch at school.

   d. Find the probability that a randomly selected person from this group buys lunch at school given that they are a junior.

   e. Find P(F) in decimal form. Round to two decimal places.

   f. Find P(B) in decimal form. Round to two decimal places.

   g. Which is greater, P(J) or P(J|L)?

   h. Which is greater, P(S|L) or P(L|S)?

   i. Find P(F|B) and explain if events F and B are independent or associated events.

4. The yearbook committee of Huntington High School is randomly selecting a student's car for the "Senior Life" section of the yearbook. If 42 of the seniors own cars, and twins Robert and Leslie each own their own cars, what is the probability that neither of their cars will be selected for the yearbook page?

5. The following Venn diagram describes cars sold during last winter at Gervy's Garage. The letter A represents air conditioning, C represents it has a CD player, and T represents automatic transmission.

    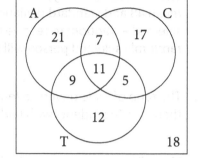

    a. How many people bought cars with air conditioning?

    b. How many people bought cars with automatic transmission and CD player?

    c. How many people purchased cars with all three options?

    d. How many people purchased cars with exactly one of these options?

    e. How many people purchased cars at Gervy's Garage last summer?

    f. A buyer from this group is selected at random to receive free satellite radio. What is the probability that they purchased the CD player?

    g. One person from this group is going to be selected at random. Find P(T).

    h. Determine if A and C are independent events and explain your answer.

    i. Examine the three shaded regions below. Describe what characteristic makes these three regions alike.

    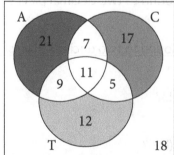

6. The distribution of weekly gasoline expenses for parents of teenagers in the Glennon Soccer Club is normally distributed with mean $46 and standard deviation 8. A parent will be selected at random. Round your answers to the nearest hundredth.

   a. What is the probability that the person spends more than $54 on gas weekly?

   b. What is the probability that the person spends less than $54 for gas weekly?

   c. What is the probability that the person spends between $22 and $70?

   d. What is the probability that the person selected spends less than $50 for gas weekly?

7. A fair, six-sided numbered cube has one of these digits on each face:

   2, 4, 6, 7, 8, 9

   a. If the cube is rolled, what is the probability of rolling an even number?

   b. What is the probability of rolling a prime number?

   c. What is the probability of rolling a number not divisible by 3?

   d. Mike rolls the die and gets a 3. He plans to roll it a second time. What is the probability of Mike rolling a 3 on the second roll?

8. The Student Council at Merrick High School is having a meeting on student parking issues for their 210 seniors. The event "goes out for lunch with their cars" is represented by L. The event "has a first period class" is represented by F. From a survey, they find out that there are 90 students who go out for lunch with their cars, 60 of which do not have a first period class. They also find out that 80 students do not go out for lunch with their cars and these 80 students also do not have a first period class. How many students have a first period class but do not take their cars out for lunch? (Hint: Draw a Venn diagram.)

4-5 Linear Automobile Depreciation

Exercises

1. Jason purchased a car for $22,995. According to his research, this make and model of car loses all of its marketable value after 9 years. If this car depreciates in a straight line form, what are the coordinates of the intercepts of the depreciation equation?

2. Suppose Phyllis knows that her car straight line depreciates at a rate of $1,997 per year over an 11-year period. What was the original price of her car?

3. Ina's car straight line depreciates at a rate of D dollars per year. Her car originally cost C dollars. What are the coordinates of the intercepts of the straight line depreciation equation?

4. A new car sells for $29,250. It straight line depreciates in 13 years. What is the slope of the straight line depreciation equation?

5. A new car straight line depreciates according to the equation $y = -1,875x + 20,625$.

    a. What is the original price of the car?

    b. How many years will it take for this car to fully straight line depreciate?

6. Write and graph a straight line depreciation equation for a car that was purchased at $27,450 and completely depreciates after 10 years.

7. Caroline purchased a car 4 years ago at a price of $28,400. According to research on this make and model, similar cars have straight line depreciated to zero value after 8 years. How much will this car be worth after 51 months?

8. The straight line depreciation equation for a luxury car is $y = -4{,}150x + 49{,}800$. In approximately how many years will the car's value drop by 30%?

9. Katie purchased a new car for $27,599. This make and model straight line depreciates for 13 years.

    a. Identify the coordinates of the x- and y-intercepts for the depreciation equation.

    b. Determine the slope of the depreciation equation.

    c. Write the straight line depreciation equation that models this situation.

    d. Draw the graph of the straight line depreciation equation.

10. Geoff purchased a used car for $16,208. This make and model used car straight line depreciates after 8 years.

    a. Identify the coordinates of the x- and y-intercepts for the depreciation equation.

    b. Determine the slope of the depreciation equation.

    c. Write the straight line depreciation equation that models this situation.

    d. Draw the graph of the straight line depreciation equation.

11. The straight line depreciation equation for a truck is $y = -4{,}265x + 59{,}710$.

    a. What is the original price of the truck?

    b. How much value does the truck lose per year?

    c. How many years will it take for the truck to totally depreciate?

12. Examine the straight line depreciation graph for a car.

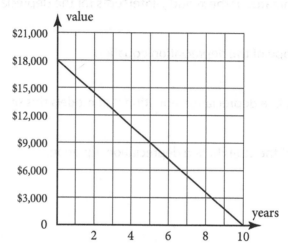

    a. At what price was the car purchased?

    b. After how many years does the car totally depreciate?

    c. Write the equation of the straight line depreciation graph shown.

13. The straight line depreciation equation for a car is $y = -2{,}682x + 32{,}184$.

    a. What is the car worth after 6 years?

    b. What is the car worth after 12 years?

    c. Suppose that T represents a length of time in years when the car still has value. Write an algebraic expression to represent the value of the car after T years.

    d. Suppose that after a years, the car depreciates to b dollars. Write an algebraic expression for a.

14. The graph of a straight line depreciation equation is shown.

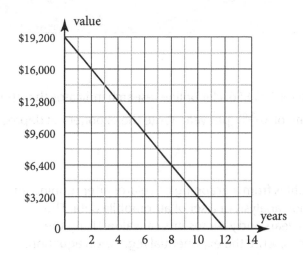

a. Use the graph to approximate the value of the car after 4 years.

b. Use the graph to approximate the value of the car after 5 years.

c. Use the graph to approximate when the car will be worth half its original value.

15. Tom purchased a new car for $36,000. He has determined that it straight line depreciates over 12 years. When he purchased the car, he made a $6,000 down payment and financed the rest with a 5-year loan where he pays $610 per month.

a. Create an expense and depreciation function where *x* represents the number of months.

b. After how many months will the amount invested in the car be equal to the value of the car? Round your answer to the nearest month.

16. Suppose that your car straight line depreciates monthly over time. You know that after 7 months your car was worth $13,200. According to an online car value calculator, after 11 months, you car is now worth $4,400. Set up an arithmetic sequence to determine how much the car depreciates each month?

4-6 Historical and Exponential Depreciation

Exercises

1. Tanya's new car sold for $23,856. Her online research indicates that the car will depreciate exponentially at a rate of $6\frac{3}{8}\%$ per year. Write the exponential depreciation formula for Tanya's car.

2. The screen to the right is from a graphing calculator after running an exponential regression analysis of a set of automobile data. The variable x represents years and y represents car value. Using the numbers on the screen, write the exponential regression equation.

```
ExpReg
 y=a*b^x
 a=43754.00259
 b=.8223288103
 r²=.8405850061
 r=-.9168342304
```

3. The screen to the right is from a graphing calculator after running an exponential regression analysis of a set of automobile data. The variable x represents years and y represents car value. What is the annual depreciation percentage for this car? Round your answer to the nearest tenth of a percent.

```
ExpReg
 y=a*b^x
 a=26092.73333
 b=.8865688485
 r².9616674348
 r=-.9806464372
```

4. Sharon purchased a used car for $24,600. The car depreciates exponentially by 8% per year. How much will the car be worth after 5 years? Round your answer to the nearest penny.

5. Brad purchased a 5-year old car for $14,200. When the car was new, it sold for $24,000. Find the depreciation rate to the nearest hundredth of a percent.

6. Lyle's new car cost him $28,000. He was told that this make and model depreciates exponentially at a rate of 11.5% per year. How much will his car be worth after 57 months?

7. Gina bought a used car for A dollars. B years ago, when the car was new, it sold for C dollars. Express the depreciation rate in terms of A, B, and C.

8. A car exponentially depreciates at a rate of 8.5% per year. Mia purchased a 4-year-old car for $17,500. What was the original price of the car when it was new? Round your answer to the nearest thousand dollars.

9. Nancy and Bob bought a used car for $22,800. When this car was new, it sold for $30,000. If the car depreciates exponentially at a rate of 9.2% per year, approximately how old is the car? Round your answer to the nearest hundredth of a year.

10. A car originally sold for $21,000. It depreciates exponentially at a rate of 6.2% per year. When purchasing the car, Jon put $5,000 down and pays $3,000 per year to pay off the balance.

    a. Write the exponential depreciation equation. Write the expense equation.

    b. Graph these two equations on the same axes.

    c. After how many years will his car value equal the amount he paid to date for the car? Round your answer to the nearest year.

    d. What is the approximate value of the car at this point? Round to the nearest hundred dollars.

11. The historical prices of a car are recorded for 14 years as shown.

Age	Value	Age	Value	Age	Value
0	21,000	5	13,105	10	8,178
1	19,110	6	11,925	11	7,448
2	17,390	7	10,852	12	6,772
3	15,825	8	9,875	13	6,163
4	14,401	9	8,987	14	5,608

    a. Use exponential regression to determine the exponential depreciation equation that models this data. Round to the nearest hundredth. Note: Due to rounding, some values might not calculate to the exact amount as shown in the table.

    b. Determine the depreciation rate.

12. Use the table of values in Exercise 11. Consider the values to represent a geometric sequence.

    a. What is the common ratio?   **b.** What is the general term for this geometric sequence?

13. The car that Dana bought is 5 years old. She paid $11,100. This make and model depreciates exponentially at a rate of 10.25% per year. What was the original price of the car when it was new? Round your answer to the nearest dollar.

14. Arnold bought a 3-year old car. He paid A dollars for it. This make and model depreciates at a rate of D percent per year. Write an expression for the original selling price of the car when it was new.

15. A new car sells for $31,400. It exponentially depreciates at a rate of 4.95% to $26,500. How long did it take for the car to depreciate to this amount? Round your answer to the nearest tenth of a year.

4-7 Driving Data

Exercises

1. A car travels at an average rate of speed of 60 miles per hour for $7\frac{1}{2}$ hours. How many miles does this car travel?

2. A car travels m miles in t hours. Express its average speed algebraically.

3. Juanita has a hybrid car that averages 44 miles per gallon. Her car has a 12-gallon tank. How far can she travel on one full tank of gas?

4. Ruth is planning a 1,543-mile trip to a math teachers' conference in San Diego. She plans to average 50 miles per hour on the trip. At that speed, for how many hours will she be driving? Express your answer to the nearest hour.

5. Lisa is a trucker and needs to keep track of her mileage for business purposes. She begins a trip with an odometer reading of x miles and ends the trip with an odometer reading of y miles.

   a. Express the total number of miles covered algebraically.

   b. If the trip takes h hours of driving, express the average speed algebraically.

   c. If the truck used g gallons of gas during the trip, express the mpg the truck averaged during the trip algebraically.

   d. If gas costs c dollars per gallon, write an algebraic expression that represents the fuel expense for the trip.

6. Abby's car gets approximately 24 miles per gallon. She is planning a 1,200-mile trip.

   a. About how many gallons of gas should she plan to buy?

   b. At an average price of $2.40 per gallon, how much should she expect to spend for gas?

7. Sarah drives at an average speed of s miles per hour for h hours. Express algebraically the number of miles she covers.

8. Raquel is driving from New York City to Daytona, Florida, a distance of 1,034 miles. How much time is saved by doing the trip at an average speed of 60 mph as compared with 55 mph? Round to the nearest half-hour.

9. Complete the table. Round entries to the nearest hundredth.

Distance (mi)	Rate (mph)	Time (hours)	MPG	Gallons Used	Price per gallon ($)	Cost for Fuel ($)
200	40	a.	b.	12	$2.33	c.
d.	55	6	20	e.	G	f.
1,000	60	g.	h.	45.4	i.	T
1,000	r	j.	x	k.	G	l.

10. Monique is away at college, and realized she left her laptop at home, 625 miles away. She arranges to meet her father at a location somewhere between home and college, so he can bring her the laptop.

    a. Monique averages 55 mph, and her part of the trip takes h hours. Represent the miles she covered algebraically.

    b. Her father takes 2 more hours than Monique to make his part of the trip, and his average speed is 50 mph. Represent the distance he covered algebraically.

    c. What is the sum of the distances they covered, expressed algebraically, using your answers from parts a and b?

    d. What is the numerical sum of the distances they covered?

    e. Write an equation that can be used to find the number of hours they traveled.

    f. How many hours did it take Monique to do her part of the trip?

    g. How many miles did Monique drive?

    h. How many hours did it take her father to do his part of the trip? How many miles did her father drive?

11. Francois' car gets about 12.5 kilometers per liter. He is planning a 1,600-kilometer trip.

    a. About how many liters of gas should Francois plan to buy? Round your answer to the nearest liter.

    b. At an average price of $0.90 US per liter, how much should Francois expect to spend for gas?

12. Ace Car Rental charges customers $0.18 per mile driven. You picked up a car and the odometer read x miles and brought it back with the odometer reading y miles. Write an algebraic expression for the total cost Ace would charge you for mileage use on a rented car.

4-8 Driving Safety Data

Exercises

Answer each hour and minute question to the nearest unit. Answer each second question to the nearest tenth.

5,280 feet = 1 mile; 1,000 meters = 1 kilometer

1. How many miles does a car traveling at 57 mph cover in one hour?

2. How many feet does a car traveling at 57 mph cover in one hour? In one minute? In one second?

3. How many miles does a car traveling at 70 mph cover in one hour?

4. How many feet does a car traveling at 70 mph cover in one hour? In one minute? In one second?

5. How many miles does a car traveling at a mph cover in one hour?

6. How many feet does a car traveling at a mph cover in one hour? In one minute? In one second?

7. How many kilometers does a car traveling at 50 kph cover in one hour?

8. How many meters does a car traveling at 50 kph cover in one hour? In one minute? In one second?

9. How many kilometers does a car traveling at a kph cover in one hour?

10. How many meters does a car traveling at a kph cover in one hour? In one minute? In one second?

11. Complete the chart:

Speed	Reaction Distance	Braking Distance
75 mph		
65 mph		
55 mph		
45 mph		
5 mph		

12. Jerry is driving 35 miles per hour as he approaches a park. A dog darts out into the street between two parked cars, and Jerry reacts in about three-quarters of a second. What is his approximate reaction distance (do not use the estimate)?

13. Manuel is driving 60 miles per hour on a state road with a 65 mph speed limit. He sees a fallen tree up ahead and must come to a quick, complete stop.

    a. What is his estimated reaction distance?

    b. What is his approximate braking distance?

    c. About how many feet does the car travel from the time he switches pedals until the car has completely stopped?

14. Anita is driving on the highway at the legal speed limit of 63 mph. She sees a police road block about 300 feet ahead and must come to a complete stop. Her reaction time is approximately $\frac{3}{4}$ of a second. Is she far enough away to safely bring the car to a complete stop? Explain your answer.

15. Rob is driving on a Canadian highway near Montreal at 63 kph. He sees an accident about 30 meters ahead and needs to bring the car to a complete stop. His reaction time is approximately $\frac{3}{4}$ of a second. Is he far enough away from the accident to safely bring the car to a complete stop?

16. Model the total stopping distance by the equation $y = \frac{x^2}{20} + x$ where x represents the speed in mph, and y represents the total stopping distance in feet.

    a. Graph this equation for the values of x where $x \geq 10$ and $x \leq 65$.

    b. Use the graph to approximate the stopping distance for a car traveling at 30 mph.

    c. Use the graph to approximate the speed for a car that completely stops after 240 feet.

17. A spreadsheet user inputs a speed in kph into cell A1.

    a. Write a formula that would enter the approximate equivalent of that speed in mph in cell A2.

    b. Write a spreadsheet formula that would enter the approximate total stopping distance in meters in cell A3.

4-9 Accident Investigation Data

Exercises

1. A car is traveling on a cement road with a drag factor of 1.1. The speed limit on this portion of the road is 45 mph. It was determined that the brakes were operating at 85% efficiency. The driver notices that the drawbridge is up ahead and that traffic is stopped. The driver immediately applies the brakes and the tires leave four distinct skid marks each 50 feet in length.

    a. What is the minimum speed the car was traveling when it entered the skid? Round your answer to the nearest tenth.

    b. Did the driver exceed the speed limit when entering the skid?

2. Highway 21 has a surface drag factor of 0.72. A car with a *b* percent braking efficiency is approaching an accident causing the driver to apply the brakes for an immediate stop. The tires leave four distinct skid marks of *c* feet each. Write an expression for determining the minimum speed of the car when entering into the skid.

3. Mark was traveling at 40 mph on a road with a drag factor of 0.85. His brakes were working at 80% efficiency. To the nearest tenth of a foot, what would you expect the average length of the skid marks to be if he applied his brakes in order to come to an immediate stop?

4. Davia is traveling on an asphalt road at 50 miles per hour when she immediately applies the brakes in order to avoid hitting a deer. The road has a drag factor of *A*, and her brakes are operating at 90% efficiency. Her car leaves three skid marks each of length *r*. Write an algebraic expression that represents the skid distance.

5. Determine the radius of the yaw mark made when brakes are immediately applied to avoid a collision based upon a yaw mark chord measuring 59.5 feet and a middle ordinate measuring 6 feet. Round your answer to the nearest tenth.

6. Arami's car left three skid marks on the road after she slammed her foot on the brake pedal to make an emergency stop. The police measured them to be 45 feet, 40 feet, and 44 feet. What skid distance will be used when calculating the skid speed formula?

7. Grace's car left four skid marks on the road surface during a highway accident. Two of the skid marks were each 52 feet, and two of the skid marks were each 56 feet. What skid distance will be used when calculating the skid speed formula?

8. Sam's car left three skid marks. Two of the marks were each *A* feet long, and one skid mark was *B* feet long. Write the algebraic expression that represents the skid distance that will be used in the skid speed formula.

9. Russell was driving on a gravel road that had a 20 mph speed limit posted. A car ahead of him pulled out from a parking lot causing Russell to immediately apply the brakes. His tires left two skid marks of lengths 60 feet and 62 feet. The road had a drag factor of 0.47. His brakes were operating at 95% efficiency. The police gave Russell a ticket for speeding. Russell insisted that he was driving under the limit. Who is correct (the police or Russell)? Explain.

10. Delia was driving on an asphalt road with a drag factor of 0.80. Her brakes were working at 78% efficiency. She hit the brakes in order to avoid a cat that ran out in front of her car. Three of her tires made skid marks of 38 feet, 42 feet, and 45 feet respectively. What was the minimum speed Delia was going at the time she went into the skid?

11. A car is traveling at 52 mph before it enters into a skid. The drag factor of the road surface is 0.86, and the braking efficiency is 88%. How long might the average skid mark be to the nearest tenth of a foot?

12. Bill is driving his car at 41 mph when he makes an emergency stop. His wheels lock and leave four skid marks of equal length. The drag factor for the road surface was 0.94, and his brakes were operating at 95% efficiency. How long might the skid marks be to the nearest foot?

13. Andrea was traveling down a road at 45 mph when she was forced to immediately apply her brakes in order to come to a complete stop. Her car left two skid marks that averaged 60 feet in length with a difference of 6 feet between them. Her brakes were operating at 90% efficiency at the time of the incident. What was the possible drag factor of this road surface? What were integer lengths of each skid mark?

14. An accident reconstructionist takes measurements of the yaw marks at the scene of an accident. What is the radius of the curve if the middle ordinate measures 5.3 feet when using a chord with a length of 39 feet? Round your answer to the nearest tenth of a foot.

15. The measure of the middle ordinate of a yaw mark is 7 feet. The radius of the arc is determined to be 64 feet. What was the length of the chord used in this situation? Round your answer to the nearest tenth of a foot.

16. The following measurements from yaw marks left at the scene of an accident were taken by police. Using a 40-foot length chord, the middle ordinate measured approximately 4 feet. The drag factor for the road surface was determined to be 0.95.

    a. Determine the radius of the curved yaw mark to the nearest tenth of a foot.

    b. Determine the minimum speed that the car was going when the skid occurred to the nearest tenth.

17. A consumer safety organization wants to test the strength of auto roof straps in crash conditions. Cargo was secured to the roof of a car at a height of 5.1 feet above the ground. The car was remotely operated and traveled at 60 mph before hitting a concrete block head-on. The researchers noticed that as soon as the front of the car hit the concrete block, the straps snapped and the cargo projected off the top of the roof in a downward half-parabolic path. Let y represent height in feet, x represent horizontal distance in feet, and t represent time in seconds in the following projectile motion equations: $y = -16.1t^2 + 5.1$ and $y = -0.0021x^2 + 5.1$.

    a. How long does it take for the cargo to hit the ground? Round your answer to the nearest hundredth of a second.

    b. What is the horizontal distance that the cargo travels? Round your answer to the nearest tenth of a foot.

5-1 Look for Employment

Exercises

1. Mitchell found a job listed in the classified ads that pays a yearly salary of $57.3K. What is the weekly salary based on this annual salary?

2. Clarissa is considering two job offers. One has an annual salary of $61.1K and the other has an annual salary of $63.4K. What is the difference in the weekly pay for these two jobs, rounded to the nearest dollar?

3. Mr. Leonard took a job through an employment agency. The job pays $88K per year. He must pay a fee to the employment agency. The fee is 22% of his first 4 weeks' pay. How much money must Mr. Leonard pay the agency, to the nearest cent?

4. The Ludwig Employment Agency posted a job in the advertising field. The fee is 18% of 3 weeks' pay. The job pays d dollars annually. Express the agency fee algebraically.

5. Arielle owns Levitt Construction Corporation. She needs a welder and is placing a seven-line classified ad. The cost of an ad that is x lines long is given by the following piecewise function. Find the cost of a seven-line ad.

    $$c(x) = \begin{cases} 33 & \text{when } x \le 4 \\ 33 + 5(x - 4) & \text{when } x > 4 \end{cases}$$

6. The *Carpenter's Chronicle* charges $12 for each of the first three lines of a classified ad and $7.25 for each additional line. Express the cost of an x-line ad, $c(x)$, algebraically as a piecewise function.

7. Job-Finder charges employers d dollars to post a job on their website. They offer a 12% discount if 10 or more jobs are posted. If 24 jobs are posted by a specific employer, write an algebraic expression for the cost of the 24 ads with the discount.

8. Art's Printing Service charges $27.50 to print 100 high-quality copies of a one-page resume. Each additional set of 100 copies costs $14.99. Express the cost, $c(r)$, of printing r sets of 100 resumes, as a piecewise function.

9. Yoko needs 300 copies of her resume printed. Dakota Printing charges $19.50 for the first 200 copies and $9 for every 100 additional copies.

    a. How much will 300 copies cost, including a sales tax of $4\frac{1}{2}$%? Round to the nearest cent.

    b. If the number of sets of 100 resumes is represented by r, express the cost of the resumes, $c(r)$, algebraically as a piecewise function.

Name _____ Date _____

10. Kim answered a help-wanted ad. The ad states that the job pays *d* dollars semiannually. Express Kim's monthly salary algebraically.

11. Rudy's job pays him $1,550 per week. Express his annual salary using the 'K' notation.

12. Teach-Tech is an online job-listing site for prospective teachers. The charge to teachers looking for jobs is $19 per week, for the first 4 weeks, to post their resumes. After four weeks, the cost is $7 per week.

    a. If *w* represents the number of weeks, represent the cost c(*w*) as a piecewise function.

    b. Find the cost of listing a resume for 8 weeks.

13. Charleen earns *m* dollars per month as a police officer. Express algebraically her annual salary using the *K* abbreviation found in classified ads.

14. Marty is a dentist. He is placing an eight-line classified ad for a hygienist. The following piecewise function gives the price of an *x*-line ad.
$$c(x) = \begin{cases} 31 & \text{when } x \le 5 \\ 20 + 6(x-5) & \text{when } x > 5 \end{cases}$$

    a. What is the cost of the first five lines if Marty purchases five lines?

    b. What is the cost of the first five lines if Marty purchases more than five lines?

    c. How much less is a six-line ad compared to a five-line ad?

15. Kevin is looking for a job as a piano technician. One classified ad lists a job that pays 64.6K. Another job he found has a weekly salary of $1,120. What is the difference in the weekly salaries of these two jobs? Round to the nearest dollar.

16. Michelle got a new job through the McCartney Employment Agency. The job pays $49,400 per year, and the agency fee is equal to 35% of one month's pay. How much must Michelle pay the agency? Round to the nearest cent.

17. Todd is looking for a job as a chemistry teacher. He plans to send resumes to 145 schools in his city. His local printer charges $34 per 100 copies and sells them only in sets of 100.

    a. How many copies must Todd purchase if he is to have enough resumes?

    b. How much will the copies cost Todd, including 5% sales tax?

5-2 | Pay Periods and Hourly Rates

Exercises

1. Mr. Varello is paid semimonthly. His annual salary is $64,333. What is his semimonthly salary, rounded to the nearest cent?

2. Mr. Whittaker earns b dollars biweekly. His employer is changing the pay procedure to monthly, but no annual salaries are changing. Express his monthly salary algebraically. $\dfrac{26b}{12}$

   $B \times 2$

3. Mrs. Frederick is paid semimonthly. Her semimonthly salary is $1,641.55. What is her annual salary?

4. Ms. Saevitz is paid semimonthly. Her annual salary is a dollars. Her office is considering going to a biweekly pay schedule. Express the difference between her biweekly salary and her semimonthly salary algebraically.

5. Julianne works as a waitress at a local Emerald Monday restaurant. Her regular hourly wage is $15.50

   a. She regularly works 40 hours per week. What is her regular weekly pay?

   b. If she works 50 weeks each year at this rate, what is her annual salary?

6. Mr. Lewis regularly works h hours per week at a rate of y dollars per hour. Express his annual salary algebraically.

7. Mrs. Roper works 40 hours per week regularly, at a rate of $16.20 per hour. When she works overtime, her rate is time and a half of her regular hourly rate. What is Mrs. Roper's hourly overtime rate?

8. If you earned d dollars per hour regularly, express your hourly overtime rate algebraically if you are paid time-and-a-half for overtime.

9. Mr. Ed earns $15.50 per hour. His regular hours are 40 hours per week, and he receives time-and-a-half overtime. Find his total pay for a week in which he works 45 hours.

10. Mrs. Trobiano regularly works 40 hours per week, at a rate of d dollars per hour. Last week she worked h overtime hours at double time. Express her total weekly salary algebraically.

11. Krissy worked her 40 regular hours last week, plus 8 overtime hours at the time-and-a-half rate. Her gross pay was $785.20. What was her hourly rate?

12. Mrs. Frasier worked her 40 regular hours last week, plus 4 overtime hours at the double-time rate. Her gross pay was $734.40. What was her hourly rate?

13. Last year Andrea's annual salary was *a* dollars, and she was paid biweekly. This year she received a raise of *r* dollars per year. She is now paid semimonthly.

   a. Express her biweekly salary last year algebraically.

   b. Express her semimonthly salary this year algebraically.

   c. How many more checks did Andrea receive each year when she was paid biweekly, as compared to the new semimonthly arrangement?

14. This week, Sean worked *h* regular hours and *t* overtime hours at the time-and-a-half rate. He earned $950. If *r* represents his hourly rate, express *r* algebraically in terms of *h* and *t*.

15. Mr. Harrison earns $32 per hour. He regularly works 40 hours per week. If he works 26 overtime hours (at time-and-a-half), would his overtime pay exceed his regular gross pay? Explain.

16. In 2003, Carlos Zambrano earned $340,000 pitching for the Chicago Cubs. In 2009, his salary was $18,750,000.

   a. Zambrano pitched in 32 games in 2003. What was his salary per game in 2003?

   b. He pitched in 28 games in 2009. What was his salary per game in 2009? Round to the nearest cent.

   c. Did he earn more per game in 2009 than he did for the entire 2003 season?

17. Last year, Mrs. Sclair's annual salary was $88,441. This year she received a raise and now earns $96,402 annually. She is paid weekly.

   a. What was her weekly salary last year? Round to the nearest cent.

   b. What is Mrs. Sclair's weekly salary this year? Round to the nearest cent.

   c. On a weekly basis, how much more does Mrs. Sclair earn as a result of her raise?

18. Leah is paid semimonthly. How many fewer paychecks does she receive in 2 years compared to someone who is paid weekly?

5-3   Commissions, Royalties, and Piecework Pay

Exercises

1. Enid wrote a textbook for high school students. She receives a 5% royalty based on the total sales of the book. The book sells for $51.95, and 12,341 copies were sold last year. How much did Enid receive in royalty payments for last year, to the nearest cent?

2. Rich wrote a novel that sells for n dollars each. He received a bonus of $50,000 to sign the contract to write the book, and he receives 9% commission on each book sale. Express the total amount of income he earns from selling b books algebraically.

3. Dafna makes sport jackets. She is paid d dollars per hour, plus a piece rate of p dollars for each jacket. Last week she made j jackets in h hours. Write an expression for her total earnings.

4. Rock singer and writer Beep Blair is paid 11.5% on her CD sales and music downloads. Last year, she sold 1.22 million CDs and 2.1 million music downloads. The CDs were sold to music stores for $5 each, and the music downloads were $1 each.

   a. What was the total amount of income from CD sales?

   b. What was the total amount of download sales?

   c. How much did Beep Blair receive in royalties last year?

5. Mr. Corona sells magazines part-time. He is paid a monthly commission. He receives 21% of his first $1,500 in sales and 14% of the balance of his sales. Last month he sold $2,233 worth of magazine subscriptions. How much commission did he earn last month?

6. Carter Cadillac pays commission to its car sales staff. They are paid a percent of the profit the dealership makes on the car, not on the selling price of the car. If the profit is less than or equal to $500, the commission rate is 18%. If the profit is greater than $500 and less than or equal to $2,000, the commission rate is 24% of the profit. If the profit is above $2,000, the rate is 27% of the profit.
   If p represents the profit, express the commission $c(p)$ algebraically as a split function.

7. Mrs. Lohrius sells electronics on commission. She receives 10% of her first x dollars in sales and 12% of the balance of her sales. Last month, she sold y dollars worth of electronics, where $y > x$. Express the commission she earned last month algebraically.

8. Abbey Road Motors pays a percent commission to its sales people. They are paid a percent of the profit the dealership makes on a car. If the profit is less than or equal to $1,000, the commission rate is 20%. If the profit is greater than $1,000 and less than or equal to $2,000, the commission rate is 20% of the first $1,000 and 24% of the remainder of the profit. If the profit is above $2,000, the rate is 20% of the first $1,000 of profit, 24% of the next $1,000 of profit, and 29% of the amount of profit over $2,000. If p represents the profit, express the commission $c(p)$ algebraically as a split function.

9. Casey is a real estate agent. She earns 8.15% commission on each sale she makes. After working with a potential buyer for $3\frac{1}{2}$ months, she finally sold a house for $877,000.

   a. What did Casey earn in commissions for this sale?

   b. This was her only sale for the entire $3\frac{1}{2}$-month period. What was her average salary per month for this period, to the nearest cent?

   c. For the next 4 months, Casey is not able to sell a house due to a faltering economy. What is her average monthly salary for the past $7\frac{1}{2}$ months, to the nearest cent?

10. Barry works at Larry's Computer Outlet. He receives a weekly salary of $310 plus 3.05% commission based on his sales. Last year, he sold $1,015,092 worth of computer equipment. How much money did Barry earn last year, to the nearest cent?

11. Jill picks corn and gets paid at a piecework rate of 55 cents per container for the first 300 containers picked. She receives 60 cents per container for every container over 300 that she picks. Last week, Jill picked 370 containers. How much did she earn?

12. Vicki works at Apple Appliances. She earns d dollars per hour, but is also paid p% commission on all sales. Last week she sold w dollars worth of appliances in the h hours she worked. Write an expression that represents her salary for the week.

13. Ms. Halloran works in a factory. She receives a salary of $15 per hour and piecework pay of 15 cents per unit produced. Last week she worked 40 hours and produced 988 units.

   a. What was her piecework pay? What was her total hourly pay for the week? What was her total pay for the week?

   b. If her boss offered to pay her a straight $18 per hour and no piecework pay for the week, would she earn more or less than under the piecework pay system?

   c. Under her current pay plan, what would her total weekly salary have been if she produced 0 units?

5-4 | Employee Benefits

Exercises

1. Ali has worked at a fashion magazine for the last 5 years. Her current annual salary is $64,000. When she was hired, she was told that she had four days of paid vacation time. For each year that she worked at the magazine, she would gain another three days of paid vacation time to a maximum of 26 days. How many paid vacation days does she now get at the end of 5 years of employment?

2. Ina's employer offers a sliding paid vacation. When she started work, she was given two paid days of vacation. For each 4-month period she stays at the job, her vacation is increased by one day.

   a. Let x represent the number of 4-month periods worked and y represent the total number of vacation days. Write an equation that models the relationship between these variables.

   b. How much vacation time will she have after working for this employer for 6.5 years?

3. When Tyler started at his current job, his employer gave him five days of paid vacation time with a promise of five additional paid vacation days for each 2-year period he remains with the company to a maximum of 5 work weeks of paid vacation time.

   a. Let x represent the number of years he has worked for this employer and y represent the number of paid vacation days he has earned. Write an equation that models the relationship of these variables.

   b. It has been 8 years since Tyler began working for this employer. How many paid vacation days has he earned?

   c. When will Tyler reach the maximum number of paid vacation days allowable?

4. When Alton started his current job, his employer told him that he had one day of paid vacation until he reaches his first year with the company. Then, at the end of the first year, he would have three vacation days. After each year, his number of vacation days would triple up to 27 days of paid vacation.

   a. Let x represent the number of years worked and y represent the number of paid vacation days. Write an equation that models the relationship between these variables.

   b. How many vacation days will he have earned after 2 years?

   c. In what year will he have maxed out his vacation days?

5. Martha's employee benefits include family health-care coverage. She contributes 18% of the cost. Martha gets paid biweekly and $108.00 is taken out of each paycheck for family health-care coverage. How much does her employer contribute annually for the family coverage?

6. Rachel contributes 20% of the cost of her individual health care. This is a $38 deduction from each of her weekly paychecks. What is the total value of her individual coverage for the year?

7. At Chocolatier Incorporated, there are two factors that determine the cost of health care. If an employee makes less than $65,000 per year, he pays $52 per month for individual coverage and $98 per month for family coverage. If an employee makes at least $65,000 per year, individual coverage is $67 per month and family coverage is $122 per month.

    a. Graham makes $62,800 per year. He has individual health care. His yearly contribution is 10% of the total cost. How much does his employer contribute?

    b. Claudia 's annual salary is $75,400. She has family health care. Her employer contributes $1,052 per month toward her total coverage cost. What percent does Claudia contribute toward the total coverage? Round to the nearest tenth of a percent.

8. Dan's employee benefits include health-care coverage. His employer covers 78% of the cost, which is a contribution of $1,599.78 toward the total coverage amount. How much does Dan pay for his coverage?

9. Liz works at *Food For Thought* magazine. Her employer offers her a pension. Liz's employer uses a formula to calculate the pension. Retiring employees receive 2.1% of their average salary over the last 4 years of employment for every year worked. Liz is planning on retiring at the end of this year after, 20 years of employment. Her salaries for the last 4 years are $66,000; $66,000; $73,000; and $75,000. Calculate Liz's annual pension.

10. As part of their employee benefits, all workers at Light and Power Electric Company receive a pension that is calculated by multiplying the number of years worked times 1.875% of the average of their three highest years' salaries. Mia has worked for LPEC for 30 years and is retiring. Her highest salaries were $92,000, $94,800, and $96,250. Calculate Mia's pension.

11. In Ben's state, the weekly unemployment compensation is 55% of the 26-week average for the two highest-salaried quarters. A quarter is three consecutive months. For July, August, and September, Ben earned a total of $22,400. In October, November, and December, he earned a total of $22,800. Determine Ben's weekly unemployment compensation.

12. Carol's weekly unemployment compensation is *W* percent of the 26-week average for the two highest salaried quarters. For January, February, and March, Carol earned *X* dollars. In April, May, and June, she earned *Y* dollars. Write an algebraic expression that represents Carol's weekly unemployment compensation.

5-5 Social Security and Medicare

Exercises

1. Dr. Grumman got his first job in 2016. In that year, the government took out 6.2% of a person's income for Social Security, until a person made $118,500. If Dr. Grumman earned $131,340 in 2016, how much did he pay to Social Security?

2. Lauren earned a total of d dollars last year, where $d < $99,000$. The government took out 6.2% for Social Security and 1.45% for Medicare. Write an algebraic expression that represents what she paid to Social Security and Medicare combined.

3. In 1978, the Social Security and Medicare rate combined was 6.05%, and this was deducted from all earnings up to a maximum taxable income of $17,700.

   a. Express the combined Social Security and Medicare tax $s(x)$ for 1978 as a piecewise function.

   b. Ten years later, the combined percent had increased to 7.51% and the maximum taxable income had increased to $45,000. Express the Social Security tax $s(x)$ for 1988 as a piecewise function.

   c. If a person earned $50,000 in 1978, and $50,000 in 1988, what was the difference in the Social Security and Medicare taxes paid?

4. In 2016, the government took out 6.2% of earnings for Social Security to a maximum taxable income of $118,500. For Medicare, 1.45% of all earnings was paid. How much money should someone have earned in 2016 so that their payments into Medicare were equal to their payments into Social Security? Round to the nearest dollar.

5. In 1998, Lisa earned $149,461.20. The Social Security maximum taxable income was $68,400, and the Social Security percent was 6.2%.

   a. What was her monthly gross pay?

   b. In what month did Lisa hit the maximum taxable Social Security income?

   c. How much Social Security tax did Lisa pay in May, to the nearest cent?

   d. How much Social Security tax did Lisa pay in July, to the nearest cent?

   e. How much Social Security tax did Lisa pay in June, to the nearest cent?

The following table gives a historical look at Social Security and Medicare taxes for the years 2000–2016. Use the table for Exercises 6–10.

Year	Social Security Percent	Social Security Maximum Taxable Income	Medicare Percent	Income Subject to Medicare Tax
2000	6.2%	76,200	1.45%	All income
2001	6.2%	80,400	1.45%	All income
2002	6.2%	84,900	1.45%	All income
2003	6.2%	87,900	1.45%	All income
2004	6.2%	87,900	1.45%	All income
2005	6.2%	90,000	1.45%	All income
2006	6.2%	94,200	1.45%	All income
2007	6.2%	97,500	1.45%	All income
2008	6.2%	102,000	1.45%	All income
2009	6.2%	106,800	1.45%	All income
2010	6.2%	106,800	1.45%	All income
2011	4.2%	106,800	1.45%	All income
2012	4.2%	110,100	1.45%	All income
2013	6.2%	113,700	1.45%	All income
2014	6.2%	117,000	1.45%	All income
2015	6.2%	118,500	1.45%	All income
2016	6.2%	118,500	1.45%	All income

6. In 2010, for the first time since 2004 the maximum taxable income was not raised. Find the maximum a person could pay into Social Security for 2010.

7. In 2011, the percent deducted for Social Security was lowered to 4.2% to help stimulate the economy. How much did a taxpayer earning more than the maximum taxable income save in 2011 due to the lower rate?

8. Let $t(x)$ represent the total combined Social Security and Medicare taxes for the year 2007. If x represents the income, express this total as a piecewise function.

9. Mr. Jackson had two jobs in 2005. The first job, in which he earned $74,007, was from January to August, and the second job, in which he earned $35,311, was from August to the end of the year. The employer for the second job took out Social Security taxes on all of Mr. Jackson's income. As a result, he paid too much Social Security tax. How much should he be refunded?

10. In 2015, Dr. Kirmser's gross pay was $381,318.60.

    a. What was her monthly gross pay?

    b. In what month did she hit the maximum taxable Social Security income?

    c. How much Social Security tax did she pay in February? Round to the nearest cent.

    d. How much Social Security tax did she pay in September? Round to the nearest cent.

    e. How much Social Security tax did Dr. Kirmser pay in April? Round to the nearest dollar.

11. Use the information from the table to examine Social Security and Medicare taxes for 2005.

    a. If x represents income, express the Social Security function $s(x)$ for 2005 as a piecewise function.

    b. Graph the Social Security function for 2005.

    c. Find the coordinates of the cusp.

    d. If x represents income, what is the Medicare function $m(x)$ for 2005?

    e. Graph the Medicare function for 2005 on the same axes as the Social Security function in part b.

    f. Elena worked three jobs in 2005. The total of her three incomes was less than $90,000. At Hamburger Coach, she made h dollars. At the Binghamton Book Exchange, she made b dollars. At Ruby's Restaurant, she made r dollars. Express the combined total of her social security and Medicare taxes as an algebraic expression.

    g. In 2005, how much money would someone have to have earned so that their payments into Medicare were equal to their payments into Social Security? Round to the nearest dollar.

6-1 Tax Tables, Worksheets, and Schedules

Exercises

Use the portion of the tax table shown here to answer Exercises 1–7.

If line 27 (taxable income) is—		And you are —				If line 27 (taxable income) is—		And you are —				If line 27 (taxable income) is—		And you are —			
At least	But less than	Single	Married filing jointly *	Married filing sepa-rately	Head of a house-hold	At least	But less than	Single	Married filing jointly *	Married filing sepa-rately	Head of a house-hold	At least	But less than	Single	Married filing jointly*	Married filing sepa-rately	Head of a house-hold
		Your tax is —						Your tax is —						Your tax is —			
77,000						**80,000**						**83,000**					
77,000	77,050	15,050	10,844	15,093	13,579	80,000	80,050	15,800	11,594	15,933	14,329	83,000	83,050	16,550	12,344	16,773	15,079
77,050	77,100	15,063	10,856	15,107	13,591	80,050	80,100	15,813	11,606	15,947	14,341	83,050	83,100	16,563	12,356	16,787	15,091
77,100	77,150	15,075	10,869	15,127	13,604	80,100	80,150	15,825	11,619	15,961	14,354	83,100	83,150	16,575	12,369	16,801	15,104
77,150	77,200	15,088	10,881	15,135	13,616	80,150	80,200	15,838	11,631	15,975	14,366	83,150	83,200	16,588	12,381	16,815	15,116
77,200	77,250	15,100	10,894	15,149	13,629	80,200	80,250	15,850	11,644	15,989	14,379	83,200	83,250	16,600	12,394	16,829	15,129
77,250	77,300	15,113	10,906	15,163	13,641	80,250	80,300	15,863	11,656	16,003	14,391	83,250	83,300	16,613	12,406	16,843	15,141
77,300	77,350	15,125	10,919	15,177	13,654	80,300	80,350	15,875	11,669	16,017	14,404	83,300	83,350	16,625	12,419	16,857	15,154
77,350	77,400	15,138	10,931	15,191	13,666	80,350	80,400	15,888	11,681	16,031	14,416	83,350	83,400	16,638	12,431	16,871	15,166
77,400	77,450	15,150	10,944	15,205	13,679	80,400	80,450	15,900	11,694	16,045	14,429	83,400	83,450	16,650	12,444	16,885	15,179
77,450	77,500	15,163	10,956	15,219	13,691	80,450	80,500	15,913	11,706	16,059	14,441	83,450	83,500	16,663	12,456	16,899	15,191
77,500	77,550	15,175	10,969	15,233	13,704	80,500	80,550	15,925	11,719	16,073	14,454	83,500	83,550	16,675	12,469	16,913	15,204
77,550	77,600	15,188	10,981	15,247	13,716	80,550	80,600	15,938	11,731	16,087	14,486	83,550	83,600	16,688	12,481	16,927	15,216
77,600	77,650	15,200	10,994	15,261	13,729	80,600	80,650	15,950	11,744	16,101	14,479	83,600	83,650	16,700	12,494	16,941	15,229
77,650	77,700	15,213	11,006	15,275	13,741	80,650	80,700	15,963	11,756	16,115	14,491	83,650	83,700	16,713	12,506	16,955	15,241
77,700	77,750	15,225	11,019	15,289	13,754	80,700	80,750	15,975	11,769	16,129	14,504	83,700	83,750	16,725	12,519	16,969	15,254
77,750	77,800	15,238	11,031	15,303	13,766	80,750	80,800	15,988	11,781	16,143	14,516	83,750	83,800	16,738	12,531	16,983	15,266
77,800	77,850	15,250	11,044	15,317	13,779	80,800	80,850	16,000	11,794	16,157	14,529	83,800	83,850	16,750	12,544	16,997	15,279
77,850	77,900	15,263	11,056	15,331	13,791	80,850	80,900	16,013	11,806	16,171	14,541	83,850	83,900	16,763	12,556	17,011	15,291
77,900	77,950	15,275	11,069	15,345	13,804	80,900	80,950	16,025	11,819	16,185	14,554	83,900	83,950	16,775	12,569	17,025	15,304
77,950	78,000	15,288	11,081	15,359	13,816	80,950	81,000	16,038	11,831	16,199	14,566	83,950	84,000	16,788	12,581	17,039	15,316

1. Abe is single. His taxable income is $83,492. How much does Abe owe in taxes?

   $ 16,663.

2. Roberta is married and filing a joint return with her husband Steve. Their combined taxable income is $80,997. How much do they owe in taxes?

   $ 11,831.

3. Quinn files as Head of Household. His tax is $14,404. What is his range of income according to the tax table?

   $ 80,300 ~ 80,350

4. Determine the tax for each filing status and taxable income amount listed.

   a. single $80,602

   $15,950

   b. head of household $83,572

   $ 15,216

   c. married filing jointly $77,777

   $ 11,031

   d. married filing separately $83,050

   $16,787.

5. Given a taxable income amount, express the tax table line that would be used in compound inequality notation.

   a. $i = \$80,154$

   i ≥ 80150 and i < 80,200

   b. $i = \$83,221$

   i ≥ 83,200 and i < 83250

6. Given the taxable income amount, express the tax table line that would be used in interval notation.

   a. $i = \$80,101$

   $80,100 \leq i < 80,150$

   b. $i = 77,686$

   $77,650 \leq i < 77,700$

7. Given the filing status and the tax, identify the taxable income interval that was used to determine that tax. Express your answer in interval notation.

   a. head of household $14,554

   $80900 \leq i < 80,950$

   b. single $15,800

   $80,000 \leq i < 80,050$

   c. married filing jointly $12,544

   $83,800 \leq i < 83,850$

   d. married filing separately $15,989

   $80,200 \leq i < 80,250$

Use the Tax Schedule for Head of Household to answer Exercises 8–12.

Schedule Z— If your filing status is **Head of household**

If your taxable income is: Over—	But not over—	The tax is:	of the amount over—
$0	$13,150	.... 10%	$0
13,150	50,200	$1,315.00 + 15%	13,150
50,200	129,600	6,872.50 + 25%	50,200
129,600	209,850	26,722.50 + 28%	129,600
209,850	411,500	49,192.50 + 33%	209,850
411,500	439,000	115,737.00 + 35%	411,500
439,000	....	125,362.00 + 39.6%	439,000

8. Calculate the tax for each of the taxable incomes of a head of household taxpayer.

   a. $200,000

   $46,434.50

   b. $23,872

   $2,923.30

   c. $121,890

   $24,795

   d. $82,251

   $14,885.25

9. For what taxable income would a taxpayer have to pay $6,872.50 in taxes?

   $50,200

10. According to the tax schedule, Ann has to pay about $40,000 in taxes. What is Ann's taxable income interval?

    $129,600 \leq i < 209,850$

11. Sam's taxable income is $92,300. What percent of his taxable income is his tax? Round to the nearest percent.

    $\approx 19\%$ 92300 $\dfrac{17397.50}{92300} = .188 = .19$

12. Manny's taxable income, t, is between $209,850 and $411,500. Write an algebraic expression that represents the amount of his tax.

Name _____ Date _____

Use the tax computation worksheet for a single taxpayer to answer Exercises 13–15.

Section A— Use if your filing status is **Single**. Complete the row below that applies to you.

Taxable income If line 43 is—	(a) Enter the amount from line 43	(b) Multiplication amount	(c) Multiply (a) by (b)	(d) Subtraction amount	Tax Subtract (d) from (c). Enter the result here and on Form 1040, line 44
At least $100,000 but not over $189,300	$	× 28% (0.28)	$	$ 6,928.75	$
Over $189,300 but not over $411,500	$	× 33% (0.33)	$	$ 16,393.75	$
Over $411,500 but not over $413,200	$	× 35% (0.35)	$	$ 24,623.75	$
Over $413,200	$	× 39.6% (0.396)	$	$ 43,630.95	$

13. Calculate the tax for each of the taxable incomes using the tax computation worksheet above.

   a. $189,000

   b. $415,221

   c. $372,951

14. Let x represent a single taxpayer's taxable income that is over $189,300 but not over $411,500. Write an expression for this taxpayer's tax in terms of x.

15. Let w represent the tax for any taxable income t on the interval $t > 413,200$. Round amounts to nearest dollar.

   a. Calculate the lowest tax on this interval.

   b. Calculate the highest tax on this interval.

   c. Express the tax for this row of the worksheet in interval notation in terms of w.

6-2 Modeling Tax Schedules

Exercises

Use the tax schedule for a married filing jointly taxpayer to answer Exercise 1.

Schedule Y-1— If your filing status is **Married filing jointly** or **Qualifying widow(er)**

If your taxable income is:		The tax is:	of the amount over—
Over—	But not over—		
$0	$18,450	········· 10%	$0
18,450	74,900	$1,845.00 + 15%	18,450
74,900	151,200	10,312.50 + 25%	74,900
151,200	230,450	29,387.50 + 28%	151,200
230,450	411,500	51,577.50 + 33%	230,450
411,500	464,850	111,324.00 + 35%	411,850
464,850	·········	129,996.50 + 39.6%	464,850

1. There are six taxable income intervals in this chart. Let x represent any taxable income. Express those intervals in tax schedule notation, interval notation, and compound inequality.

Tax Schedule Notation	Interval Notation	Compound Inequality Notation

2. Let y represent the tax and x represent the taxable income of a head of household taxpayer. Use the tax worksheet below to write four equations in $y = mx + b$ form for values of x that are greater than or equal to $100,000.

Section D— Use if your filing status is **Head of household**. Complete the row below that applies to you.

Taxable income If line 43 is—	(a) Enter the amount from line 43	(b) Multiplication amount	(c) Multiply (a) by (b)	(d) Subtraction amount	Tax Subtract (d) from (c). Enter the result here and on Form 1040, line 44
At least $100,000 but not over $129,600	$	× 25% (0.25)	$	$ 5,677.50	$
Over $129,600 but not over $209,850	$	× 28% (0.28)	$	$ 9,565.50	$
Over $209,850 but not over $411,500	$	× 33% (0.33)	$	$ 20,058.00	$
Over $411,500 but not over $439,000	$	× 35% (0.35)	$	$ 28,288.00	$
Over $413,200	$	× 39.6% (0.396)	$	$ 48,482.00	$

3. Write a piecewise function to represent the tax $f(x)$ for the first three taxable income intervals in the schedule below for a single taxpayer.

Schedule X— If your filing status is **Single**

If your taxable income is: Over—	But not over—	The tax is:	of the amount over—
$0	$9,225	·········· 10%	$0
9,225	37,450	$922.50 + 15%	9,225
37,450	90,750	5,156.25 + 25%	37,450
90,750	189,300	18,481.25 + 28%	90,750
189,300	411,500	46,075.25 + 33%	189,300
411,500	413,200	119,401.25 + 35%	411,500
413,200	··········	119,996.25 + 39.6%	413,200

4. Examine the tax schedule for the years 1914 and 2015. The schedule in 1914 applied to all taxpayers. The schedule for 2015 is for a single taxpayer. **Marginal Tax Rate** is the rate of tax a taxpayer pays at his/her income level.

1914			2015		
Marginal Tax Rate	**Tax Brackets**		**Marginal Tax Rate**	**Tax Brackets**	
	Over	**But not over**		**Over**	**But not over**
1.0%	$0	$20,000	10.0%	$0	$9,275
2.0%	$20,000	$50,000	15.0%	$9,275	$37,650
3.0%	$50,000	$75,000	25.0%	$37,650	$91,150
4.0%	$75,000	$100,000	28.0%	$91,150	$190,150
5.0%	$100,000	$250,000	33.0%	$190,150	$413,350
6.0%	$250,000	$500,000	35.0%	$413,350	$415,050
7.0%	$500,000		39.6%	$415,050	

a. What was the marginal tax rate for a taxpayer with a taxable income of $40,000 in 1914?

b. What was the marginal tax rate for a taxpayer with a taxable income of $40,000 in 2015?

c. Based on the marginal tax rate, find the difference in tax between a single taxpayer in 1914 making $90,000 and a single taxpayer in 2015 making the same amount.

5. Examine the following piecewise function that models the tax computation worksheet for a single taxpayer. Write the tax equations in $y = mx + b$ form.

$$c(x) = \begin{cases} 14,652.50 + 0.28(x - 71,950) & 100,000 < x \le 150,150 \\ 36,548.50 + 0.33(x - 150,150) & 150,150 < x \le 326,450 \\ 94,727.50 + 0.35(x - 326,450) & x > 326,450 \end{cases}$$

6-3 | Income Statements

Exercises

1. Jack's employer just switched to a new payroll system. He wants to make sure that his net pay has been computed correctly. His gross pay per pay period is $587.34. He has the following deductions: Social Security tax (6.2%), Medicare tax (1.45%), federal withholding tax $164.45, state withholding tax $76.34, retirement insurance contribution $50.00, disability insurance fee $8.00, medical insurance fee $23.00, and dental insurance fee $8.00. What should his net pay be for this pay period?

2. Tony makes an hourly salary of $15.40 for 40 regular hours of work. For any time worked beyond 40 hours, he is paid at a rate of time-and-a-half per hour. Last week, Tony worked 46 hours. Find each of the following for this period.

   a. Tony's gross pay

   b. Social Security tax

   c. Medicare tax

3. Elizabeth works for Picasso Paint Supplies. Her annual salary is $72,580.

   a. What is Elizabeth's annual Social Security deduction?

   b. What is Elizabeth's annual Medicare deduction?

   c. Elizabeth is paid every other week. What is her biweekly gross pay?

   d. Each pay period, Elizabeth's employer deducts 21% for federal withholding tax. What is the total amount withheld for federal tax from Elizabeth's annual salary?

   e. If Elizabeth is taxed at an annual rate of 2.875% for city tax, how much is deducted from her salary per paycheck to withhold that tax?

   f. As of January 1, Elizabeth will receive a 9.1% raise. What will Elizabeth's annual salary be?

4. A taxpayer's annual Social Security tax is $6,107. What is the taxpayer's gross annual salary?

5. A taxpayer's annual Medicare tax is $841. What is the taxpayer's gross annual salary?

6. Let x represent the gross paycheck amount for a weekly pay period. Let y represent the number of the week in the year (1 = first week, 2 = second week, etc.)

   a. Write an expression to represent the calendar year-to-date amount.

   b. Write an expression for the Social Security tax for each pay period.

   c. Write an expression for the year-to-date Social Security tax.

   d. Write an expression for the Medicare tax for each pay period.

   e. Write an expression for the year-to-date Medicare tax.

   f. If C percent of the gross pay is withheld for federal taxes, write an expression for the weekly amount withheld for those taxes.

   g. Write an expression for the total annual federal tax withheld.

7. Use the partial information given in this electronic W-2 form to calculate the amount in Box 3.

1 Wages, tips, other compensation	2 Federal income tax withheld
3 Social security wages	4 Social security tax withheld **$6,361.20**
5 Medicare wages and tips	6 Medicare tax withheld
7 Social security tips	8 Allocated tips
9 Advance EIC payment	10 Dependent care benefits
11 Nonqualified plans	12a See instructions for box 12 E **$2,400.00**
13 Statutory employee / Retirement plan [X] / Third-party sick pay	12b
14 Other caf125 **$5,600.00**	12c

8. Melanie is taxed at a 19% tax rate for her federal taxes. Last year, she reduced her taxable income by contributing X dollars per biweekly paycheck to her tax deferred retirement account and Y dollars per biweekly paycheck to her FSA. Write an expression for the amount she reduced her taxes by if her gross biweekly pay is Z dollars.

9. Examine Alfredo Plata's incomplete W-2 form. Based on the information determine the amounts in each of the following boxes.

   a. Box 1

   b. Box 3

   c. Box 4

   d. Box 5

a Employee's social security number **000-00-0000**	OMB No. 1545-0008	Safe, accurate, FAST! Use	Visit the IRS website at www.irs.gov/efile.
b Employer identification number (EIN) **00-0000000**		1 Wages, tips, other compensation	2 Federal income tax withheld **$14,662.50**
c Employer's name, address, and ZIP code **Blake Industries 234 Washington Blvd Seven Bridges, NY 10515**		3 Social security wages	4 Social security tax withheld
		5 Medicare wages and tips	6 Medicare tax withheld **$1,346.04**
		7 Social security tips	8 Allocated tips
d Control number		9 Advance EIC payment	10 Dependent care benefits
e Employee's first name and initial **Alfredo** Last name **Plata** Suff.		11 Nonqualified plans	12a See instructions for box 12 E **$2,300.00**
13 Statutory employee / Retirement plan [X] / Third-party sick pay		12b	
137 Michigan Rd. Seven Bridges, NY 10515		14 Other caf125 **$4,280.00**	12c
			12d
f Employee's address and ZIP code			
15 State Employer's state ID number **00-0000000**	16 State wages, tips, etc.	17 State income tax	18 Local wages, tips, etc.	19 Local income tax	20 Locality name

6-4 Forms 1040EZ and 1040A

Exercises

1. Arthur's employer withheld $15,987.76 in federal income tax. After completing his return, Arthur has determined that his tax is $18,945.22. Will Art get a refund, or does he owe the IRS and how much?

2. Latoya is an accountant who also works as a part-time museum tour guide. Information from her tax worksheet includes wages from the accounting job, $85,290.45; wages from the museum job, $12,670.34; interest, $563.99; and dividends, $234.67. What is Latoya's total income?

3. Drew is single with a taxable income for last year of $83,472. His employer withheld $16,998 in federal taxes.

   a. Use the tax tables from Section 6-1 in this workbook to determine Drew's tax.

   b. Does Drew get a refund?

   c. Find the difference between Drew's tax and the amount withheld by his employer.

4. Davia and Bill are married and file their taxes jointly. Davia's taxable income was $50,675 and Bill's was $32,802. Davia's employer withheld $11,654 in federal taxes. Bill's employer withheld $7,345 in federal taxes.

   a. What is their combined taxable income?

   b. Use the tax tables from section 6-1 in this workbook to determine their tax.

   c. Do they get a refund?

   d. Find the difference between their tax and the amount withheld by their employers.

5. Parker is single and paying off his graduate student loan. The monthly payment is $679.34. He is hoping to receive an income tax refund that is large enough to make at least one monthly payment. His taxable income is $77,911 and his employer withheld $19,458 in federal taxes.

   a. Use the tax tables from section 6-1 of this workbook. How much of a refund will Parker receive?

   b. How many loan payments will Parker be able to make with this refund?

Financial Algebra Workbook 6-4

6. Eileen is a married taxpayer who files jointly with her husband. Their combined taxable income is *X* dollars and their tax is *Y* dollars. Eileen's employer withheld *A* dollars from her salary and her husband's employer withheld *B* dollars from his salary during the year.

   a. Write an algebraic expression for the amount they would receive should they get a refund.

   b. Write an algebraic expression for the amount they would owe in taxes if the combined amount withheld was not enough to cover the tax they owe.

Use the current applicable 1040EZ or 1040A tax form and the IRS information booklet that goes with each to complete a tax return. Tax forms are available at www.irs.gov.

7. Gil Anderson is single and works as a manager of a local print shop. Use his W-2 form below to complete a 1040EZ form.

a Employee's social security number 000-00-0000			
b Employer identification number (EIN) 00-0000000	1 Wages, tips, other compensation $76,854.00	2 Federal income tax withheld $18,449.00	
c Employer's name, address, and ZIP code	3 Social security wages $76,854.00	4 Social security tax withheld $4,764.95	
River Road Printing 79 River Road Cliff, Idaho 83319	5 Medicare wages and tips $76,854.00	6 Medicare tax withheld $1,114.38	
	7 Social security tips	8 Allocated tips	
d Control number	9 Advance EIC payment	10 Dependent care benefits	
e Employee's first name and initial / Last name Gilbert R. Anderson	11 Nonqualified plans	12a See instructions for box 12	
246 Edwards Street Cliff, Idaho 83319	13 Statutory employee / Retirement plan / Third-party sick pay	12b	
	14 Other	12c	
		12d	
f Employee's address and ZIP code			
15 State / Employer's state ID number 00-0000000	16 State wages, tips, etc. $76,854.00	17 State income tax $8,456.14	18 Local wages, tips, etc. / 19 Local income tax / 20 Locality name

8. Pat and Rosa Invidia are married with three children. Rosa is a seamstress and Pat is a salesman. Complete a 1040A form using the information on their W-2 forms below. Pat and Rosa received $987.21 in interest on bank deposits and $230 in stock dividends.

a Employee's social security number 000-00-0000			
b Employer identification number (EIN) 00-0000000	1 Wages, tips, other compensation $48,031.00	2 Federal income tax withheld $10,566.82	
c Employer's name, address, and ZIP code	3 Social security wages $48,031.00	4 Social security tax withheld $2,977.92	
Brooklyn Clothiers 8 Bushwick Street Brooklyn, NY 11202	5 Medicare wages and tips $48,031.00	6 Medicare tax withheld $696.45	
	7 Social security tips	8 Allocated tips	
d Control number	9 Advance EIC payment	10 Dependent care benefits	
e Employee's first name and initial / Last name Patrick A. Invidia	11 Nonqualified plans	12a See instructions for box 12	
10 Presidential Street Brooklyn, NY 11201	13 Statutory employee / Retirement plan / Third-party sick pay	12b	
	14 Other	12c	
		12d	
f Employee's address and ZIP code			
15 State / Employer's state ID number 00-0000000	16 State wages, tips, etc. $48,031.00	17 State income tax $5,283.41	18 Local wages, tips, etc. $48,031.00 / 19 Local income tax $3,362.17 / 20 Locality name

a Employee's social security number 000-00-0000			
b Employer identification number (EIN) 00-0000000	1 Wages, tips, other compensation $48,121.00	2 Federal income tax withheld $9,143.00	
c Employer's name, address, and ZIP code	3 Social security wages $48,121.00	4 Social security tax withheld $2,983.50	
Fresh Fashions 221 Memorial Drive New York, NY 10025	5 Medicare wages and tips $48,121.00	6 Medicare tax withheld $697.75	
	7 Social security tips	8 Allocated tips	
d Control number	9 Advance EIC payment	10 Dependent care benefits	
e Employee's first name and initial / Last name Rosa S. Invidia	11 Nonqualified plans	12a See instructions for box 12	
10 Presidential Street Brooklyn, NY 11201	13 Statutory employee / Retirement plan / Third-party sick pay	12b	
	14 Other	12c	
		12d	
f Employee's address and ZIP code			
15 State / Employer's state ID number 00-0000000	16 State wages, tips, etc. $48,121.00	17 State income tax $5,293.31	18 Local wages, tips, etc. $48,121.00 / 19 Local income tax $3,368.47 / 20 Locality name

6-5   Form 1040 and Schedules A and B

Exercises

1. Mike and Lisa Lerner had combined wages of $91,301 last year. They also had a bank interest of $792 and $667. They received stock dividends of $287 and $530. During the year, Lisa won a $1,000 prize. Find the total income from wages, bank interest, dividends, and the prize.

2. Paul and Mary had $78,111.19 in income from their jobs and their bank interest. They also had $2,139 worth of moving expenses, and Paul paid $6,000 in alimony. These two expenses are deductions from income. Find their adjusted gross income.

3. The Starkey family had a total income of i dollars. They also had a dollars in adjustments to income. Express their adjusted gross income algebraically.

4. The Kivetsky family had an adjusted gross income of $119,245.61. They included medical deductions on Schedule A. They had $14,191 in medical expenses. Medical insurance covered 80% of these expenses. The IRS allows medical and dental expenses deductions for the amount that exceeds 10% of a taxpayer's adjusted gross income. How much can they claim as a medical deduction?

5. Anita's adjusted gross income was a dollars last year. The IRS allows medical and dental expense deductions for the amount that exceeds 10% of a taxpayer's adjusted gross income. If she had m dollars of medical expenses last year, and 80% of these expenses were covered by her insurance, express her medical expense deduction algebraically.

6. The Mazzeo family donated c dollars in cash to charity last tax year. They also donated b bags of used clothing valued at $50 each. They donated two used computers valued at x dollars each to the local food pantry. Express their total charitable contributions algebraically.

7. The Holfester family took $5\frac{1}{2}$ hours to gather information for their Schedule A. The itemized deductions saved them $4,095 in taxes. What was the mean savings per hour to fill out Schedule A? Round to the nearest dollar.

8. The Lowatsky family had $9,441 worth of hurricane damage that was not covered by insurance. They need to follow IRS procedures to take a casualty deduction on Schedule A.

   a. The IRS requires that $100 be deducted from each casualty. What is the total casualty loss after the $100 is deducted?

   b. Their adjusted gross income is $67,481. Find 10% of their adjusted gross income.

   c. Their Schedule A casualty deduction can be found by subtracting 10% of the adjusted gross income from the answer to part a. What is their casualty loss deduction?

9. Maria's adjusted gross income was *a* dollars. She had three different casualties last year that were not covered by insurance. A laptop computer valued at *x* dollars was taken from her gym locker, and her car was stolen, and she did not have comprehensive insurance, so she lost *y* dollars. An ice storm caused *z* dollars worth of damage that was not covered by insurance. Express her casualty loss algebraically.

10. The Filipowitz family consists of two parents and four children, and one grandparent that lives with them. If the deduction per exemption is *e* dollars, express their total deduction for exemptions algebraically.

11. Jenny and Larry Strawberry are married with two children. They have health insurance. Their W-2 forms for the last completed tax year are shown below. They also had the following tax-related information.

Bank interest	$636	Dividends	$129
Real estate taxes	$7,444	Mortgage interest paid	$6,211
Casualty and theft loss	$14,200	Job expenses	$815

Charity contributions cash, $570; used clothing, $330

Medical expenses (not reimbursed by insurance) $288; $3,240; $976; $399

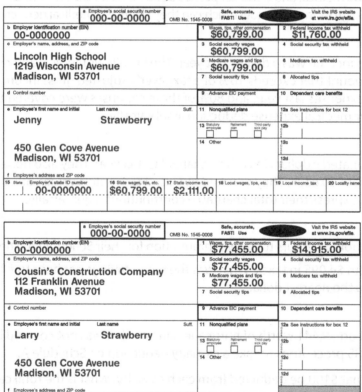

a. Download the most recent Form 1040, and complete it, including Schedules A and B. Jenny and Larry are married filing a joint return. Round all entries to the nearest dollar.

b. Find in the missing Social Security and Medicare taxes from their W-2's.

7-1   Find a Place to Live

Exercises

1. Use the interval 25%–30% to find the monetary range that is recommended for the monthly housing budget in each situation. Round to the nearest dollar.

    a. Enrique makes $109,992 per year.   b. Barbara makes $5,000 per month.

2. Hannah's financial advisor believes that she should spend no more than 26% of her gross monthly income for housing. She has determined that amount is $1,794 per month. Based on this amount and her advisor's recommendation, what is Hannah's annual salary?

3. Adina makes $53,112 per year and is looking to find a new apartment rental in her city. She searched online and found an apartment for $1,500 per month. The recommendation is to budget between 25% and 30% of your monthly income for rent. Can Adina afford this apartment based upon the recommended interval? Explain.

4. Rex makes $12.50 per hour. He works 35 hours a week. He pays 24% of his gross earnings in federal and state taxes and saves 10% of his monthly gross income. He is considering renting an apartment that will cost $1,600 per month.

    a. Is this monthly rental fee within the recommended 25%–30% housing expense range?

    b. Based upon his expenses, can he make the monthly payments?

5. Brian's monthly gross income is $2,950. He pays 22% of his monthly gross earnings in federal and state taxes and spends 10% of that monthly income to pay off his credit card debt. Brian is also paying off a loan his parents gave him for a new car by sending them 8% of his income per month. Brian found an apartment near his work that rents for $1,300 per month. Will he be able to make the payments without changing the amounts he pays toward his loan and credit card debt?

6. Larry is renting an apartment that will cost r dollars per month. He must pay a D dollars application fee and C dollars for a credit application. His security deposit is two month's rent and he must also pay the last month's rent upon signing the lease. His broker charges 7% of the total year's rent as the fee for finding the apartment. Write an algebraic expression that represents the total cost of signing the lease.

7. The square footage and monthly rental of 10 similar one-bedroom apartments yield the linear regression $y = 0.775x + 950.25$ where x represents the square footage of the apartment and y represents the monthly rental price. Grace can afford $1,500 per month rent. Using the equation, what size apartment should she expect to be able to rent for that price?

8. Carla wants to rent a new apartment. She made a table listing the square footage of the apartments and their rents as shown. Use linear regression analysis to determine if there is a correlation between the square footage (x) and the amount charged for the monthly rent (y).

Square feet (x)	600	790	800	850	925	980	1,050	1,400
Monthly Rent (y)	$795	$1,523	$1,600	$1,800	$2,000	$2,100	$2,300	$3,000

a. What is the linear regression equation? Round the numbers to the nearest hundredth.

b. Interpret the correlation coefficient.

9. The square footage and monthly rental of 15 similar one-bedroom apartments yield the linear regression formula $y = 1.3485x + 840.51$, where x represents the square footage and y represents the monthly rental price. Round answers to the nearest whole number.

a. Determine the monthly rent for an apartment with 1,200 square feet.

b. Determine the square footage of an apartment with a monthly rent of $1,900.

10. Conan is moving into a two-bedroom apartment in Valley Oaks. The monthly rent is $2,000. His up-front fees are shown. How much can he expect to pay up front for this apartment?

> **Application fee:** 3% of one month's rent
> **Credit application fee:** $20
> **Security deposit:** 1 month's rent and last month's rent
> **Broker's fee:** 14% of year's rent

11. Debbie wants to rent a one-bedroom apartment in April Acres. The apartment has a monthly rent of D dollars. The fees are shown below. Write an algebraic expression that represents the amount she is expected to pay before renting the apartment.

> Application fee: 2% of one month's rent
> Last month's rent paid up front
> Security deposit: $\frac{1}{2}$ month's rent
> Broker's fee: 4% of one year's rent

12. NuHome Movers charges $95 per hour for loading/unloading services and $80 per hour for packing/unpacking services. Their charge is $2.50 per mile for truck rental. Jay is moving a distance of 200 miles and needs 9 hours of loading/unloading and 7 hours of packing/unpacking. What will his moving cost be if the service also charges 7.25% tax on the total?

13. iVan charges an hourly rate for a moving team to load and unload a truck. The charge is a different hourly rate for a team to pack and unpack boxes. Use the quotes to determine the iVan hourly rates.

Weekday Move	Weekend Move
8 hours of loading/unloading	5 hours of loading/unloading
6 hours of packing/unpacking	3 hours of packing/unpacking
$890 total cost	$515 total cost

7-2 Read a Floor Plan

Exercises

1. The length of a room is $19\frac{1}{2}$ feet. When using $\frac{1}{4}$ inch = 1 foot scale, what would be the length of the wall on a floor plan?

2. Kim is building a large gazebo for her backyard. It is in the shape of a regular hexagon. Each side of the gazebo is 12 feet long. The apothem is 10.4 feet. She needs to purchase stones for the floor. It costs $9.50 per square foot for a special type of interlocking stone. Find the cost of the gazebo's floor. Round to the nearest ten dollars.

3. Find the volume of a rectangular room that measures 13 feet by 15.5 feet, with an 8-foot ceiling.

4. A rectangular room has length L and width W. Its volume is 2,455 cubic feet. Express the height of the ceiling algebraically in terms of x.

5. A regular heptagon (7 sides) has perimeter 126 and area A. Express the apothem a of the heptagon algebraically in terms of the area A.

6. An irregular plane figure drawn on graph paper is framed inside of a 15 by 40 rectangle. To find its area, 10,000 random points are generated, and 5,710 of them land inside the irregular region. What is the area of the irregular region, to the nearest integer?

7. The main meeting room of the Glen Oaks Community Center measures 46 feet by 34 feet and has a 12-foot ceiling. It is well insulated and faces the east side of his house. The manager wants to purchase an air conditioner. How large an air conditioner should he purchase? Round up to the next thousand BTUs.

8. Circle O is situated in rectangle ACDE as shown.

   a. Find the area of the rectangle.

   b. Find the radius of the circle.

   c. Find the area of the circle to the nearest integer.

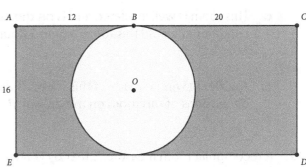

   d. Find the area of the shaded region.

9. Kyoko plans to put a new wood floor in her den, which is shown in the floor plan.

Den
17 ft × 14.5 ft

a. What is the area of the floor?

b. At a cost of $11 per square foot, how much will it cost to put down the new floor?

c. Kyoko plans to put a rectangular area rug in the room. The rug will be large enough so that only a 2-foot wide section of the wood floor will be exposed on each side. Find the dimensions of the area rug.

d. What is the area of the area rug?

e. Find the area of the wood floor that will be exposed once the area rug is laid down.

10. A rectangular room has length *L*, width *W*, and height *H*, where *L*, *W*, and *H* are measured in feet.

a. Express the volume in cubic feet algebraically.

b. If carpeting costs $72 per square yard, write an expression for the cost of carpeting the floor of this room.

11. A rectangular room measures 16 feet by 18 feet. The ceiling is 9 feet high.

a. Find the total area of the four walls in the room.

b. If a gallon of paint costs $37.99 and it covers 400 square feet on average, what is the cost of painting the room, including the ceiling, with two coats of paint? Explain your answer.

c. This room is well insulated and is on the north side of the house. How large of an air conditioner would this room require? Round to the next highest thousand BTUs.

d. A scale drawing is made of this room using the scale 1 sq ft = $\frac{1}{4}$ sq in. What are the dimensions of this room on the drawing?

12. A rectangular room measures *L* feet by *W* feet. The ceiling is 8 feet high. The walls and the ceiling will be painted the same color. Express the total area of the walls and ceiling algebraically.

7-3 Mortgage Application Process

Exercises

1. The Jacobs family is planning to buy a home. They have some money for a down payment already. They see a home they like and compute that they would need to borrow $213,000 from a bank over a 30-year period. The APR is 3.75%.

   a. What is the monthly payment, to the nearest cent?

   b. What is the total of all of the monthly payments over the 30 years?

   c. What is her total interest for the 30 years?

2. Pam and Chris found a home for which they would have to borrow H dollars. If they take out a 25-year loan with monthly payment M, express the interest I in terms of H and M.

3. A bank requires that the Dotkoms pay their homeowner's insurance, property taxes, and mortgage in one monthly payment to the bank. If their monthly mortgage payment is $1,711.22, their semi-annual property tax bill is $3,239, and their annual homeowner's insurance bill is $980, how much do they pay the bank each month?

4. If you borrow $200,000 at an APR of 4% for 25 years, you will pay more per month than if you borrow the money for 30 years at 4%.

   a. What is the monthly payment on the 25-year mortgage, to the nearest cent?

   b. What is the total interest paid on the 25-year mortgage?

   c. What is the monthly payment on the 30-year mortgage?

   d. What is the total interest paid on the 30-year mortgage?

   e. How much more interest is paid on the 30-year loan? Round to the nearest dollar.

   f. What is the difference between the monthly payments of the two different loans? Round to the nearest dollar.

5. The assessed value of the Kreiner family's house is $457,000. The annual property tax rate is 2.66% of assessed value. What is the annual property tax on the Kreiner's home?

6. Tom and Gwen have an adjusted gross income of $144,112. Their monthly mortgage payment for the house they want would be $1,483. Their annual property taxes would be $9,330, and the homeowner's insurance premium would cost them $1,099 per year. They have a monthly $444 car payment, and their credit card monthly payment averages $4,021.

   a. Based on the front-end ratio, would the bank lend them $220,000 to purchase the house they want? Explain your answer.

   b. Based on the back-end ratio, would the bank lend them $220,000 to purchase the house they want? Explain your answer.

7. The market value of Jennifer and Neil's home is $319,000. The assessed value is $280,000. The annual property tax rate is $19.70 per $1,000 of assessed value.

   a. What is the property tax on their home?

   b. How much do they pay monthly toward property taxes? Round to the nearest cent.

8. Rowena has an adjusted gross income of k dollars. She is looking at a new house. Her monthly mortgage payment would be m. The annual property taxes would be p, and the annual homeowner's premium would be h. Express her front-end ratio algebraically.

9. Britney and Jakob have an annual adjusted gross income of x dollars. Their monthly mortgage payment is m. Their annual property taxes are p, and their annual homeowner's premium is h. They have a monthly credit card bill of c and a monthly car loan of l. They also have an annual college tuition bill represented by t. Write an expression for each ratio.

   a. front-end ratio   b. back-end ratio

10. Find the monthly payment (before the balloon payment) for a 25-year, interest-only balloon mortgage for $300,000 at an APR of 3.1%. Round to the nearest ten dollars.

11. An interest-only balloon mortgage of a principal p for 20 years has total interest of i dollars. Write an expression for the amount of each monthly payment before the balloon payment.

12. Ted has an adjusted gross income of $120,006. He wants a house with a monthly mortgage payment of $1,921 and annual property taxes of $7,112. His semiannual homeowner's premium would be $897. Ted has a credit card bill that averages $300 per month.

   a. What is the back-end ratio to the nearest percent? The front-end ratio?

   b. Assume that his credit rating is good. Based on the back-end ratio, would the bank offer him a loan? Explain.

   c. Based on the front-end ratio, would the bank offer him a loan? Explain.

7-4 | Purchase a Home

Exercises

1. Let L represent a loan amount, P represent the percent of the APR on that loan, D represent the daily interest that would be charged on the loan at that rate, M represent the number of days in a month, and C represent the closing date on a loan.

   a. If I represents the interest on the loan for one year, write an algebraic expression for the interest I.

   b. Write an algebraic expression for the daily interest in terms of I.

   c. Let Z represent the interest due on a loan from the closing date to the end of the month. Write an algebraic expression for Z.

2. Liz and Nick are buying a $725,000 home. They have been approved for a 3.25% APR, 30-year mortgage. They made a 20% down payment and will be closing on March 11.

   a. What is their interest on the loan for one year?

   b. What is the daily interest?

   c. How much should they expect to pay in prepaid interest at the closing?

3. How much will be charged in prepaid interest on a $500,000 loan with an APR of 3.725% that was closed on August 26?

4. Lars has been approved for a $420,000, 20-year mortgage with an APR of 5.125%.

   a. What is his monthly payment?

   b. How much interest would he expect to pay on the loan in the first month?

   c. How much of that monthly payment will go toward the principal?

5. The bank approved Sylvie for a $250,000, 15-year mortgage with an APR of 3.95%.

   a. What is her monthly payment?

   b. How much interest would she expect to pay on the loan in the first month?

   c. How much of that monthly payment will go toward the principal?

6. Hillary was told that based on the price of her home, her approximated closing costs would range from $11,600 to $40,600. How much was the price of her home?

7. Laura and Rich have been approved for a $325,000, 15-year mortgage with an APR of 5.3%. Using the mortgage and interest formulas, complete the two-month amortization table.

Payment Number	Beginning Balance	Monthly Payment	Toward Interest	Toward Principal	Ending Balance
1					
2					

8. Examine the following loan amortization table for the first 5 months of a $475,000, 25-year mortgage with an APR of 5.45%. Complete the table.

Payment Number	Beginning Balance	Monthly Payment	Toward Interest	Toward Principal	Ending Balance
1	475,000.00		2,157.29	745.46	474,254.54
2			2,153.91	748.84	473,505.70
3	473,505.70			752.24	472,753.46
4	472,753.46		2,147.09		471,997.80
5	471,997.80	2,902.75	2,143.66	759.09	
6	471,238.71	2,902.75	2,140.21		470,476.17

9. Examine the loan amortization table for months 92–95 of a $200,000, 8-year mortgage with an APR of 5.025%. Determine the amounts missing in the table.

Payment Number	Beginning Balance	Monthly Payment	Toward Interest	Toward Principal	Ending Balance
92	12,514.18		52.40	2,481.97	
93	10,032.21		42.01	2,492.36	7,539.85
94			31.57	2,502.80	5,037.05
95	5,037.05			2,513.28	2,523.77

10. Shay took out a $560,000, 10-year mortgage with an APR of 3.5%. The first month she made an extra payment of $1,200. What was the ending balance at the end of her first month?

11. Randy took out an adjustable rate mortgage for $375,000 over 20 years. It had an introductory rate of 3.25% for the first year, and then it rose to 4.5%. Complete the chart for the 13th payment.

Payment Number	Beginning Balance	Monthly Payment	Toward Interest	Toward Principal	Ending Balance
12	362,608.15	2,126.98	982.06	1,144.92	361,463.23
13					

7-5 Points

Exercises

1. Determine the cost of the points and the new interest rate for each loan amount and interest rate. Assume each point costs 1% of the loan amount.

    a. $280,000, original APR 4.18%, 1 point with a 0.2% discount

    b. $350,000, original APR 2.95%, 2 points with a 0.275% discount per point.

    c. $600,000, original APR 4.6%, 3 points with a 0.225% discount per point.

    d. $450,000, original APR 3.75%, 1 point with a 0.3% discount

    e. $2,000,000, original APR 3.55%, 2 points with a 0.235% discount per point.

2. Juanita wants to take out a 15-year, $350,000 loan with a 3.4% APR. She is not sure as to whether or not she should purchase points to reduce the loan APR. If she purchases two points, it will decrease her APR by 0.125% per point. Each point will cost 1% of her loan. Compare her monthly payments with and without the purchase of the points.

3. Ansel was approved for an 18-year, $450,000 loan with a 3.9% APR. If he purchases 1 point, his APR will reduce to 3.7%. How much will his monthly payment savings be?

4. Akiko purchased 4 points, each of which reduced her APR by 0.165%. Each point cost 1% of her loan value. Her new APR is 2.8% and the points cost her $19,200.

    a. What was the original APR?

    b. What is her principal?

5. Hamed purchased x points. Each point lowered his APR by y%. The cost per point was z% of the loan amount. His new APR is A% and his points cost him B dollars. Write an algebraic expression for

    a. the original APR

    b. the principal

6. The Bedford Shore Credit Union offered Patti a $220,000 30-year mortgage at 3.17%. The credit union offers up to 4 points that will reduce her APR by 0.25% per point. Each point will cost 1% of the loan value. Patti is considering buying 3 points.

   a. Calculate her monthly payments with the points.

   b. Calculate her monthly payments without the points.

   c. Determine the breakeven month.

7. National Savings Bank approved Caroline for a $300,000 12-year loan at a 3.875% APR. Should Caroline purchase 1 point or no points? Each point lowers the APR by 0.125% and costs 1% of the loan amount. Justify your reasoning.

8. Alena wants to take out a $600,000 loan to purchase a new waterfront home. The bank offers a 30-year loan with an APR of 4.15%. If she purchases one point for 1% of the value of the loan, she will reduce her APR by 0.3%.

   a. What is her monthly savings with the point purchase?

   b. When will she break even?

9. Technical Savings Bank offers borrowers a zero closing cost loan. Each negative point reduces the closing costs by 1% of the principal and increases the APR by 0.125%. Jared wants to borrow $540,000 from Technical Savings at 3.48% for 25 years. The estimated closing costs are $10,000.

   a. How many negative points does he need to have a zero closing cost loan?

   b. What will his new APR be on the loan?

   c. There is a chance that in 15 years, his company may be moving to a different state. Are these negative points worth the investment?

10. Teachers' Federal Credit Union offers a 3.25%, 10-year mortgage. Moira wants to borrow $380,000 and "purchase" enough negative points to eliminate her $14,000 closing costs. Each negative point reduces the closing costs by 1% of the principal and increases the APR by 0.135%.

    a. How many points will she need?

    b. What will her new APR be?

    c. What is the breakeven time for Moira's loan?

7-6 Rentals, Condominiums, and Cooperatives

Exercises

1. On March 1, Antonio purchased a new condominium. He pays a monthly maintenance fee of $1,030. His monthly property taxes equal 13.5% of the monthly fee. How much will Anton pay in property taxes for this calendar year?

2. Sarah purchased a condominium at Tulip Meadows. She pays $3,196.80 in property taxes each year. These taxes are taken out of her monthly maintenance fee of $1,480. What percentage of this monthly fee goes to property taxes?

3. Last year, one-fifth of the Fitzgerald's $800 dollar monthly co-op maintenance fee went toward property taxes. How much property tax did the Fitzgerald's pay last year?

4. Luella's monthly maintenance fee is $720, of which p percent is tax deductible for property tax purposes. Express the annual property tax deduction algebraically.

5. The Sea Cottage Cooperative is owned by the shareholders. The co-op has a total of 32,000 shares. Linda has an apartment at Sea Cottage and owns 480 shares of the cooperative. What percentage of Sea Cottage does Linda own?

6. Last year, p percent of Shannon's x-dollar co-op monthly maintenance fee went toward property taxes. Write an algebraic expression for Shannon's annual property taxes.

7. Petra has a co-op in Sunset Village. The cooperative consists of a total of 28,000 shares. If Petra owns s shares, what percentage of the cooperative corporation does she own?

8. The South Hills Apartment Complex has just announced rate increases. All rents will increase by 3.2%, and the security deposit, which was formerly 50% of one month's rent, must now equal 60% of the new rent. Eddie rented an apartment for $1,600. In what amount should he write a check to cover the new rent and the extra security deposit?

9. Joey rented an apartment from a landlord in his hometown. His rent was R dollars per month until he moved out last week. The new tenants pay N dollars per month. Write an algebraic expression to represent the percent increase.

10. In 1998, Ben bought a co-op for $120,000. He borrowed $90,000 from the bank to make the purchase. Now he wants to sell the co-op, but the market value has decreased to $80,000. His equity in the co-op is $46,800. If he sells the co-op, he will have to pay off the mortgage. How much will he make after he pays off the mortgage?

11. Nick moved into an apartment in the city. He pays $3,200 rent per month. The landlord told him the rent has increased 3% per year on average.

   a. Express the rent y as an exponential function of the number of years x.

   b. Suppose the rent had increased $100 each year. Express the rent y as a function of the number of years x.

   c. Determine the predicted rent after 5 years using each of the two equations.

12. The monthly rents for Jillian's one-bedroom apartment, at the North Haven Towers, for a 10-year period, are given in the table.

   a. Write the exponential regression equation that models these rents. Round the numbers to the nearest hundredth.

   b. According to your equation, what is the approximate yearly rent increase percentage?

   c. Using your equation, what will the rent be in 15 years?

Year	Monthly Rent ($)
1	1,680
2	1,700
3	1,750
4	1,790
5	1,825
6	1,855
7	1,885
8	1,920
9	1,965
10	2,000

13. Beth moved into an apartment close to her new job. She will be paying $2,000 per month in rent and expects a 2.5% rent increase each year.

   a. Express the rent y as an exponential function of the number of years rented, x.

   b. What can she expect the rent to be in the 10th year?

14. Monthly rent at The Breakers Co-ops has increased annually, modeled by the exponential equation $y = 2,700(1.045)^x$. What was the percent increase per year?

15. Margot bought a condominium at a time when prices were at their highest. She paid $185,000. Since then, she has watched the market value decrease by 5% per year.

   a. Write an exponential depreciation equation to model this situation.

   b. Based on your equation, approximately when will her condominium be worth less than $145,000?

7-7   Home Maintenance and Improvement

Exercises

1. Ruth is setting up the locations of the corners of a 10' by 24' rectangular deck she is going to build in her backyard. To make sure she has a perfect rectangle, she checks to make sure the diagonals are the same.

    a. What should the length of each diagonal be?

    b. What angle does the diagonal make with the longer side of the deck? Round to the nearest degree.

    c. What angle does the diagonal make with the shorter side of the deck? Round to the nearest degree.

2. Jake is installing a staircase so his children can have access to a tree house he built. The rise of the stairs is 7 inches and the run of each stair is 10 inches. What is the slope of the staircase, expressed as a fraction?

3. The Golf King Driving Range is installing a huge net to catch long golf drives. The poles to hold the net up are 50 feet high. The contractor needs to run a wire from the top of the pole to the ground to keep the poles and the net secure. This wire is called a *guy wire*.

    a. If the guy wire runs from the top of the pole to a point on the ground 22 feet from the base of the pole, how long must the guy wire be? Round up to the next highest foot.

    b. What is the slope of the guy wire, expressed as a fraction?

4. Bill bought a set of car ramps so he can work under his car. He drives the car up the ramp and then the wheel sits on top of the shaded rectangle, as shown in the picture.

    a. If side MA has length 9 inches, what is the slope of the ramp, expressed as a fraction?

    b. If side MA has length 9 inches, what is the angle of elevation, <R, of the ramp? Round to the nearest degree.

Financial Algebra Workbook 7-7   **121**

5. A side view of Rajan's roof is shown in the diagram below.

    a. What is the length of the run of the roof?

    b. What is the pitch of the roof?

    c. Rajan plans to clean out his gutters, located at
        G, and he needs to purchase a ladder long
        enough. If the recommended angle of
        elevation for the ladder is 66 degrees, how far
        must he place the foot of the ladder from the
        house to clean his gutters? Round to the
        nearest tenth.

    d. How long a ladder must Rajan purchase? Round to the next highest foot.

6. Mark has a tree in his backyard that he wants to make sure cannot fall on his neighbor's house if
    there is a bad storm. The tree is 49 feet from his neighbor's house. From a point on the ground
    35 feet from the tree, the angle of elevation of the top of the tree is 50 degrees. How tall is the
    tree? Round to the nearest foot.

7. The Glen Head Girl Scout troop is planning to build a ramp for a local park. The Americans with
    Disabilities Act (ADA) states that handicap ramps for wheelchairs should have a slope of 1/12 or
    less. A diagram of the ramp is shown below,

    a. Convert the 22-foot horizontal length into inches.

    b. What, in inches, is the maximum height, BC, the ramp can be to adhere to ADA guidelines?
        Round to the nearest tenth of an inch.

    c. If BC has length 9 inches, what is the slope of the ramp?

    d. If BC has length 10 inches, what is the angle of elevation of the ramp? Round to the nearest
        tenth.

8. The Fickman Construction Company is building a rectangular deck that measures 40' by 20'. They need to run an electric line across the diagonal, underneath the deck. How long is the diagonal of the deck, to the nearest foot?

9. The Wright family purchased a portable movie screen for their backyard. It is held up with poles and guy wires on each side of the screen, as shown in the diagram.

a. If AE = 6 feet, what is the angle of elevation of the guy wire AD? Round to the nearest degree.

b. What is the length of the guy wire? Round to the nearest tenth.

c. How much wire is needed for the two guy wires?

d. How long is AB?

10. From a point 30 feet from the base of a tree, the angle of elevation is 65 degrees, as shown in the diagram. The eye level height is 6 feet.

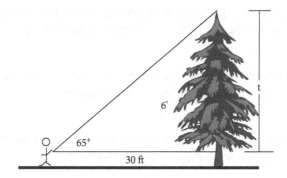

a. Find the value of t to the nearest foot.

b. Find the height of the tree, to the nearest foot.

Financial Algebra Workbook 7-7

8-1 | Business Organizations

Exercises

1. Avril invested $60,000 in a partnership with Lane, Jules, Ray, Ravi, and Petra. The total investment of all partners was $320,000. What percent of the business does Avril own?

2. The Metropolitan Corporation has issued a total of 2,400,000 shares. The North Side Investment Group owns 7.5% of those shares. How many shares does North Side own?

3. Enid, Eve, and Tammy have formed a partnership. The total investment was $400,000. Enid owns 35.4% and Eve owns 28.8% of the partnership. How much did Tammy invest?

4. Three partners are investing a total of $1,200,000 in a new restaurant. Their investments are in the ratio of 6:8:11. How much did each invest?

5. Alli, Beth, Catie, Dave, Eddie, Franny, and George invested $4,914,000 in a business venture in the ratio of 1:2:3:4:5:6:7 respectively. How much did Alli and George each invest?

6. Dennis owns 24% of a partnership. Bob owns 48% of the partnership. If Rich is the third partner, what percent of the partnership does he own? Write a simplified ratio to represent their investments in the partnership.

7. Angel owns five-eighths of a partnership in a bakery.
   a. What percent of the bakery does Angel own?

   b. Angel's partner, Lisa, owns the remaining portion of the bakery. Write a simplified ratio to represent Angel's ownership to Lisa's ownership in the bakery.

8. Austen owns seven-sixteenths of a jewelry store. The total investment for the store was $832,000. What is the value of Austen's share of the business?

9. Penny owns five-ninths of a movie theater. Penny's investment is worth $450,000. What is the total investment that was made for the movie theater?

10. The Barnaby Corporation issued 2,700,000 shares of stock at its beginning to shareholders. How many shares must a shareowner own to have a majority of the shares?

11. Ella owns 15% of Fitz Incorporated. The rest of the shares are owned equally by the remaining 5 shareholders. What percent of the corporation does each of the other shareholders own?

12. Clinton and Barbara are the partners in a local music shop. They needed $448,500 to start the business. They invested in the ratio of 11:12.

    a. How much money did each invest?

    b. What percent of the business is owned by Clinton? Round to the nearest tenth of a percent.

13. Andrea, Dina, and Lindsay invested in a partnership in the ratio of 7:9:14, respectively. Ten years later, their partnership was worth $1,800,000. Dina decided to move to Europe and sold her part of the partnership to Andrea.

    a. How much did Andrea pay Dina for her share of the partnership? Round to the nearest dollar.

    b. What percent of the business did Andrea own after she bought out Dina? Round to the nearest tenth of a percent.

    c. What was the new ratio of ownership once the business was owned by only Andrea and Lindsay?

14. Mike, Rob, Jon, and Kristy own shares in the Arlington Partnership in the ratio of $a:b:c:d$ respectively. Arlington is now worth E dollars.

    a. Write an algebraic expression for the percent of the partnership that represents Mike's investment.

    b. Jon decides to sell his portion of the partnership to Kristy. Write the new ratio of ownership for Mike, Rob, and Kristy.

    c. Write an algebraic expression for the new percent representing Kristy's ownership.

15. Fifty-five and one-half percent of the shareholders in a fast food chain are under the age of 40. If the corporation is owned by 86,000 investors, how many of the shareholders are 40 and over?

16. The North Salem Stock Club owns x percent of the shares of a certain corporation. Each of the 10 club members owns y shares of that stock. The corporation's ownership is represented by a total of S shares of stock. Express the number of shares of the corporation owned by each club member algebraically.

17. A partnership owned by 25 partners is worth 5.4 million dollars. The partnership loses a lawsuit worth 6.2 million dollars. How much of the settlement is each partner liable for after the partnership is sold? Explain.

8-2 | Stock Market Data

Exercises

1. Use the trading data for Friday, October 20 and Friday, October 27 to answer the questions.

Discovery Group	
October 20	
Last	$38.50
Trade Time	4:00 P.M. ET
Chg	$1.56
Open	$37.22
52-week High	$76.19
52-week Low	$22.78
Sales in 100s	19,700
High	$40.10
Low	$36.77

Discovery Group	
October 27	
Last	$42.00
Trade Time	4:00 P.M. ET
Chg	$1.50
Open	$42.50
52-week High	$76.19
52-week Low	$22.78
Sales in 100s	23,600
High	$42.50
Low	$42.00

a. What was the difference between the high and the low prices on October 20?

b. On October 27, what was the actual volume of Discovery Group shares posted? Write the volume in numerals.

c. At what price did Discovery Group close on October 19?

d. Use the October 19 closing price from above and the October 20 opening price to find the difference in prices as a percent increase. Round to the nearest hundredth percent.

e. On October 21, Discovery Group announced that they would close one of their manufacturing plants. This resulted in a drop in their stock price. It closed at $32. Express the net change from October 20 to October 21 as a percent, rounded to the nearest tenth of a percent.

f. On October 28, Discovery Group announced that they would not be closing the plant. This news caused the price of their stock to rise. It closed at $48.20. Express the net change from October 27 to October 28 as a percent, rounded to the nearest tenth of a percent.

g. Explain why the 52-week high and 52-week low numbers are the same in both charts.

h. Examine the closing price of Discovery Group on October 27. One year earlier, one share closed at 30% higher than that amount. What was the closing price one year earlier?

Name_____ Date_____

2. Write each of the following volumes using complete numerals.

   a. Sales in 100s: 82,567

   b. Sales in 100s: 321.78

   c. Sales in 1000s: 12,856

   d. Sales in 10,000s: 6,478.98

   e. Sales in 100,000s: 35,495.235

   f. Sales in 100,000: 3.2

Use the spreadsheet to answer the Exercises 3–7. Use the left side of the equation to indicate in which cell to store the formula.

	A	B	C	D	E	F	G	H
1	Symbol	Stock	Aug. 21 Last	Change	% Change from Aug. 20	Aug. 20 Close	Volume in 100s	Volume in 1000s
2	ABC	American Bicycle Corp.	34.89	3.02		31.87	12345	
3	DEF	Detroit Energy Fund	8.56	0.35	4.3		121	
4	GHI	General Hospital Incorporated	14.7	−0.28		14.98	8123	
5	JKL	Juniper Kansas Luxuries	121.45	−2.95			763542	
6	MNO	Middle Network Offices	75		−0.6	75.45	2637	
7	PQR	Prince Queen Resalers	11.29	0.88				239.478
8	STU	Southern Texas Underwriters	54.92	−3.37				23754.2
9	VWX	Valley Windmill Xperience, Inc.			−1.83	64.88		493004

3. Write a formula that will convert the volume given in 100s into a volume given in 1000s.
   a. Juniper Kansas

   b. Detroit Energy

4. Write a formula that will store the exact volume for each stock in column I.
   a. Valley Windmill

   b. Middle Network

5. Write a formula to determine the close on August 20 for each of the following.
   a. Southern Texas

   b. Prince Queen Resalers

6. Write a formula to determine the percent change for each of the following.
   a. ABC

   b. GHI

7. Calculate each net change.
   a. MNO

   b. VWX

Name _____ Date _____

Exercises

Use the stock chart to answer the exercises below for December 14–18.

1. Which day had the highest price? Which day had the least low price?

2. Approximately how many shares of Lombard Incorporated were traded over the five days?

3. On what date did the stock close at a price lower than it opened?

4. Find each price.

   a. opening on December 16   **b.** high on December 18

   c. low on December 14   **d.** closing on December 15

5. Express each net change as a monetary amount and as a percent to the nearest tenth.

   a. from December 14 to December 15   **b.** from December 17 to December 18

6. Approximately how many fewer shares were traded on December 18 than on December 16?

Name _____ Date _____

Use the candlestick chart to answer the exercises below for December 14–18.

7. On which days were opening prices higher than the closing prices?

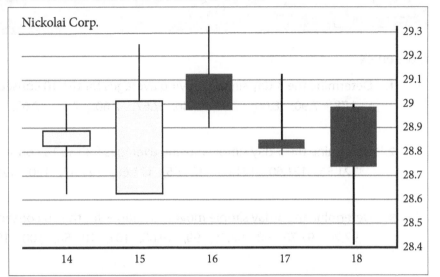

8. On which days were the closing prices higher than the opening prices?

9. On 12/16, what was the approximate closing price? approximate lowest price?

10. What was the difference between the lowest and highest prices recorded for this period?

11. What does the absence of a line at the bottom of the December 15 bar indicate?

12. Construct a bar chart for the following 5-day period, December 14–December 18.

Day	Open	Close	High	Low	Volume
14	15.98	15.95	16.07	15.93	41,000,000
15	15.83	15.75	16.01	15.65	80,000,000
16	15.80	15.69	15.85	15.67	75,000,000
17	15.59	15.80	15.95	15.56	70,000,000
18	15.91	15.59	15.91	15.59	80,000,000

8-4 Trends In Stock Closing Prices

Exercises

1. Determine the 3-day simple moving averages for the 10 consecutive day closing prices.

   7.78, 7.90, 8.00, 7.97, 7.86, 7.67, 7.60, 7.65, 7.65, 7.70

2. Determine the 5-day simple moving averages for the 10 consecutive day closing prices.

   121.56, 121.60, 121.65, 121.65, 121.60, 121.52, 120, 120.67, 121.50, 121.45

3. Determine the 6-day simple moving averages for the 10 consecutive day closing prices.

   97.70, 97.70, 98, 98.45, 99, 99.68, 101, 101.50, 100, 100.56

4. Determine the 7-day simple moving averages for the 14 consecutive day closing prices for Exxon Mobil listed.

   43.23, 43.23, 43.21, 43, 43.50, 43.55, 43.45, 43.56, 43.76, 44, 44.03, 44.09, 44, 44.02

Determine the simple moving averages (SMA) by subtraction and addition for each set of 10 consecutive day closing prices.

5. 3-day SMA

   $11.97, $11.85, $11.52, $13.17, $14.24
   $15.02, $15.26, $14.96, $13.56, $13.38

6. 4-day SMA

   $26.31, $25.94, $27.65, $27.13, $26.81
   $26.65, $26.55, $25.89, $25.82, $25.87

7. 5-day SMA

   $221.49, $222.15, $221.70, $223.81, $223.00
   $223.03, $222.99, $224.04, $224.12, $224.16

8. 6-day SMA

   $0.65, $0.53, $0.60, $0.63, $0.50,
   $0.55, $0.56, $0.58, $0.59, $0.67

9. Use a spreadsheet to determine the 10-day simple moving averages for General Electric.

17-Sep	16.97	24-Sep	17.06	1-Oct	16.31	8-Oct	16.46	15-Oct	16.79
18-Sep	16.88	25-Sep	16.35	2-Oct	15.45	9-Oct	16.20	16-Oct	16.35
21-Sep	16.43	28-Sep	16.47	5-Oct	15.59	12-Oct	16.36	19-Oct	16.05
22-Sep	17.06	29-Sep	16.91	6-Oct	16.14	13-Oct	16.32	20-Oct	15.80
23-Sep	17.17	30-Sep	16.83	7-Oct	16.03	14-Oct	16.77	21-Oct	15.51

10. Use a spreadsheet to determine the 12-day simple moving averages for Motorola.

4-Aug	7.24	10-Aug	7.17	14-Aug	7.26	20-Aug	7.37	26-Aug	7.48
5-Aug	7.13	11-Aug	7.03	17-Aug	7.06	21-Aug	7.58	27-Aug	7.34
6-Aug	7.11	12-Aug	7.07	18-Aug	7.21	24-Aug	7.48	28-Aug	7.21
7-Aug	7.13	13-Aug	7.28	19-Aug	7.29	25-Aug	7.53	31-Aug	7.18

11. The closing prices for 10 consecutive trading days for a particular stock are given here. Calculate the 5-day simple moving averages and plot both the closing prices and the averages on a graph.

15.19, 15.21, 15.32, 15.40, 15.40, 15.38, 15.41, 15.50, 15.55, 15.47

12. Discuss the implication of the crossover on the 4th day in the graph.

13. Examine the following SMA graph to determine an implication for each crossover.

a. on Day 3

b. on Day 5

c. on Day 9

14. Examine the closing prices for 15 consecutive trading days of PDGN.

Trading Day	CLOSE
1	89.67
2	89.5
3	90.12
4	90.69
5	91
6	91.1
7	91.05
8	92.75
9	93
10	94.2
11	94
12	94.9
13	94.95
14	95
15	95.1

a. Determine a linear regression equation that fits the data. Round numbers to the nearest hundredth.

b. Determine a quadratic regression equation that fits this data. Round numbers to the nearest thousandth.

c. Use the equations you found in parts a and b to determine the predicted closing price on the 16th trading day. The actual closing price was $95.99. Which regression equation was a better predictor?

8-5 | Stock Market Ticker

Exercises

Use the following ticker to answer Exercises 1–6. The stock symbols represent the corporations: C, CitiGroup Inc; BAC, Bank of America; F, Ford Motor Corp; and MSI, Motorola Solutions.

> MSI 4.2K @ 72.59 ▼0.16   BAC .65K @ 15.28 ▲1.11
>
> F 61.8K @ 13.67 ▼2.07 C 76K @ 43.54 ▲0.09

1. Millie is following the trades of Motorola Solutions. The result of the latest trade is posted on the ticker.

    a. How many shares of MSI were traded and at what price per share?

    b. What was the value of the MSI trade?

    c. Suppose the next MSI trade represents a sale of 1,200 shares at a price that is $0.23 lower than the last transaction. What will Millie see scrolling on the ticker for this transaction?

2. Susan sold her Bank of America shares as indicated on the ticker above.

    a. How many shares did she sell?

    b. For how much did each share sell?

    c. What was the total value of all the shares Susan sold?

    d. Suppose that the next BAC trade that comes across the ticker represents a sale of 34,000 shares at a price that is $2.31 higher than the last transaction. What will Susan see scrolling across her screen for this transaction of BAC?

3. How many shares of Ford are indicated on the ticker?

4. What is the total value of all of the CitiGroup shares traded?

5. Interpret each of the following.

    a. @43.54   b. MSI 4.2K   c. ▲1.11

6. What was the previous day's closing price for each stock?

7. Ron knows that JP Morgan Chase & Co has the ticker symbol JPM. What can Ron learn from the following line of symbols: JPM 0.26K @ 43.43 ▼ 0.98?

8. For their 16th birthday, Liz gave her twin daughters, Adriana and Marina, 3,500 shares of IBM to be split evenly between them. Ten years later, on September 13, the twins sold all of the shares at a price of $127.91. The closing price of IBM on September 12 was $126.13. How did this trade appear on the stock ticker?

9. Jenna contacted her broker and asked him to sell all 4,000 of her Pepsico (PEP) shares on Friday as soon as the trading price hit $59.48 per share. Jenna knew that PEP closed at $58 on Thursday. How will her trade appear on the ticker?

Use the following ticker information to answer Exercises 10–14. The stock symbols represent the corporations: BMY, Bristol-Myers Squibb; AA, Alcoa; INTC, Intel Corp; and MSFT, Microsoft.

BMY 0.88K @ 62.87 ▼ 0.93   AA 78K @ 10.73 ▲ 1.12

INTC 17.9K @ 32.09 ▼ 1.06   MSFT 0.81K @ 53.52 ▲ 2.23

10. Lucinda put in an order for some shares of Bristol-Myers Squibb.

a. As shown on the ticker, how many shares did Lucinda buy and for what price per share?

b. What was the value of Lucinda's trade?

11. Jared has sold his shares of Intel, as indicated on the above ticker.

a. How many shares did he sell and for what price per share?

b. What was the total value of all the shares Jared sold?

12. How many shares of Alcoa are indicated on the ticker?

13. What is the total value of all of the Microsoft shares traded?

14. Interpret each of the following.

a. AA 1.1K   **b.** ▼1.06   **c.** @10.73

15. Write the ticker symbols for each situation.

a. 1,500 shares of RJS at a price of $13.19, which is $0.92, lower than the previous day's close.

b. 38,700 shares of EPZ at $39.22, which is $1.83 higher than the previous day's close.

8-6 Stock Transactions

Exercises

1. Five years ago, Julianne purchased stock for $9,433. Yesterday, she sold the stock for $10,219. What was her gross capital gain?

2. A few years ago, Melky bought 100 shares of a cologne company's stock for $16.77 per share. Last month she sold all of the shares for $11.88 per share. What was her loss?

3. In March of 2009, Jennifer bought shares of stock in the Pepsi-Cola Company for $47 per share. In March 2016, she sold them for $101 per share. Express the increase in price as a percent of the purchase price. Round to the nearest tenth of a percent.

4. Mike bought shares of a brand new corporation that manufactures dish antennas. He bought the stock years ago for $4,100. He recently sold this stock for $7,100. Express his capital gain as a percent of the original purchase price. Round to the nearest tenth of a percent.

5. Fran bought shares in a supermarket chain in early 2016 for $21.11 per share. She sold them later in that same year for $20 per share. Express her loss as a percent of the purchase price. Round to the nearest percent.

6. Andy bought 300 shares of a corporation that manufactures kitchen cabinets. He bought the stock years ago for x dollars. He recently sold this stock for y dollars. Express his capital gain as a percent of the original purchase price algebraically.

7. Ashley bought $1,200 worth of stock in a home improvement store. She does not know what she will sell it for, so let x represent the selling price of all the shares. Express the percent value of Ashley's capital gain algebraically.

8. Jake bought 540 shares of Sound Foundations stock years ago for $44.50 per share. He sold them yesterday for $49.54 per share.

   a. What was the percent increase in the price per share, rounded to the nearest percent?

   b. What was the percent capital gain for the 540 shares, rounded to the nearest percent?

9. Lisa bought h shares of Home Depot stock for x dollars per share. She sold all of the shares years later for y dollars per share. Express her capital gain algebraically.

10. Jack bought w shares of Xerox stock for a total of t dollars. Write an expression for the price he paid per share.

11. Bill purchased shares of Apple for *a* dollars per share. He plans to sell them as soon as the price rises 20%. Express the price he will sell his shares at algebraically.

12. Maria purchased 1,000 shares of stock for $65.50 per share in 2009. She sold them in 2016 for $55.10 per share. Express her loss as a percent of the purchase price, rounded to the nearest tenth of a percent.

13. Allen purchased shares of stock for *x* dollars in 2016. He sold them weeks later for *y* dollars per share. Express his capital gain as a percent of the purchase price.

14. Anna bought 350 shares of stock for *p* dollars per share. She sold them last week for *s* dollars per share. Express her capital gain algebraically in terms of *p* and *s*.

15. Max bought *x* shares of stock for *y* dollars per share. His broker told him to sell them when they earn a *p* percent capital gain. Express the total selling price of the shares algebraically.

16. Donnie bought *x* shares of stock for *y* dollars per share years ago. His stock rose in price, and eventually hit a price that would earn him a 137% capital gain. He decided to sell 75% of his *x* shares.

  a. Represent 75% of the *x* shares algebraically.

  b. Represent the capital gain earned on each of the shares that were sold algebraically.

  c. Represent the capital gain earned on all of the shares that were sold algebraically.

  d. Represent the total value of the shares that were sold algebraically.

  e. Years later, the company stock falls to its lowest price of $3 per share. Donnie sells the rest of his shares. Write an expression for the total selling price of all the shares sold at $3.

17. Fill in the missing purchase prices and selling prices for stock trades in the table.

Number of Shares	Purchase Price per Share	Selling Price per Share	Capital Gain or Loss	Percent Gain or Loss (nearest tenth of a percent)
500	$54	$62	**a.**	**b.**
100	**c.**	$12	$700	**d.**
650	$31	**e.**	**f.**	15% (gain)
1,300	**g.**	$23	−$7,800	**h.**

8-7 Stock Transaction Fees

Exercises

1. Juaquin made three trades through his online discount broker, Electro-Trade. Electro-Trade charges a fee of x dollars per trade. Juaquin's first purchase was for $2,456 without the fee, his second purchase was for $3,000 without the fee, and his third purchase was for $2,119 without the fee. If the total of the purchases was $7,623 including broker fees, what does Electro-Trade charge per trade?

2. Ted made x transactions last month using Trades-Are-Us online brokers, which charges y dollars per trade. Each transaction was a sale of stock. The total value of all the shares Ted sold was t dollars. The brokers sold the stock, took out their fees, and sent Ted a check for the rest of the money he was owed. Express the value of the check Ted received from the broker algebraically.

3. The fee schedule for the Glen Head Brokerage Firm is shown in the table below.

Fee Schedule for Glen Head Brokerage Firm	Online Trades	Telephone Trades (automated)	Trades Using a Broker
Portfolio Value less than $100,000	x dollars per trade	online fee plus r dollars	c percent commission plus online fee
Portfolio Value greater than $100,000	y dollars per trade	online fee plus q dollars	p percent of commission plus online fee

   a. Joy purchased s dollars worth of stock using a broker from Glen Head Brokerage Firm. The current value of her portfolio is $21,771. Express algebraically the broker fee she must pay for this transaction.

   b. Jonathan has a portfolio worth 1.1 million dollars. He made w automated telephone trades during the past year, buying and selling $90,000 worth of stock. Express his total broker fee algebraically.

4. Meghan purchases $41,655 worth of stock on her broker's advice and pays her broker a 1.5% broker fee. She sells it when it increases to $47,300, months later, and uses a discount broker who charges $19 per trade. Compute her net proceeds after the broker fees are taken out. Round to the nearest dollar.

5. Fred is a broker who charges 1% per stock transaction. A competing online broker charges $26 per trade. If someone is planning to purchase stock, at what purchase price would Fred's commission be the same as the online broker fee?

6. Barbara purchased stock last year for $8,500 and paid a 1.25% broker fee. She sold it for $7,324 and had to pay a 0.5% broker fee. Compute her net proceeds.

7. Adam purchased stock several years ago for x dollars and had to pay a 1.5% broker fee. He sold that stock last month for y dollars and paid a discount broker $15 for the sale. Express his net proceeds algebraically.

8. Steven purchases x dollars worth of stock on his broker's advice and pays his broker a flat $12 broker fee. The value of the shares falls to f dollars months later, and Steven uses a broker who charges 1% commission to make the sale. Express his net proceeds algebraically.

9. Rich bought 20,000 dollars worth of stock and paid a y percent commission. Dan purchased 17,000 dollars worth of stock and paid a q percent commission. Find a value of y and a value of q, where y and q are each less than 3, such that Rich's commission is less than Dan's.

10. If you bought 600 shares of stock for $41 per share, paid a 1% commission, and then sold them 6 months later for $41.75 per share, with a $30 flat fee, are your net proceeds positive or negative? Explain.

11. Mr. Wankel bought x shares of stock for y dollars per share last month. He paid his broker a flat fee of $14. He sold the stock this month for p dollars per share, and paid his broker a 2% commission. Express his net proceeds algebraically.

12. Michelle Miranda Investing charges their customers a 1% commission. The Halloran Group, a discount broker, charges $13.75 per trade. For what dollar amount of stock would Miranda charge double the commission of Halloran?

13. CoronaCorp, a discount broker, charges their customers x dollars per trade. The Sclair Bear & Bull House charges a 1.5% commission. For what value of stock would both brokers charge the same commission? Express your answer algebraically.

14. Mrs. Cowley purchases $32,000 worth of stock on her broker's advice and pays her broker a 0.75% broker fee. She is forced to sell it when it falls to $25,100 two years later, and uses a discount broker who charges $17 per trade. Compute her net loss after the broker fees are taken out.

15. Sal bought x shares of a stock that sold for $31.50 per share. He paid a 1% commission on the sale. The total cost of his investment, including the broker fee, was $5,726.70. How many shares did he purchase?

16. Mrs. Didamo purchased stock years ago for d dollars and had to pay a flat $20 broker fee. The price dropped but she needed money for college so she sold it at a loss, for x dollars, plus a 1% broker fee. Express her net loss algebraically.

8-8 | Stock Splits

Exercises

1. Yesterday the Rockville Corporation instituted a 2-for-1 stock split. Before the split, the market share price was $63.44 per share and the corporation had 2.3 billion shares outstanding.

   a. What was the pre-split market cap for Rockville?

   b. What was the post-split number of shares outstanding for Rockville?

   c. What was the post-split market price per share for Rockville?

2. Suppose that a corporation has a market capitalization of $97,000,000,000 with 450M outstanding shares. Calculate the price per share to the nearest cent.

3. Tele-Mart instituted a 5-for-1 split in April. After the split, Roberta owned 1,860 shares. How many shares had she owned before the split?

4. In May, the Black Oyster Corporation instituted a 3-for-1 split. After the split, the price of one share was x dollars. What was the pre-split price per share, expressed algebraically?

5. Patterson's Appliances was considering a 2-for-3 reverse split. If the pre-split market cap was $634,000,000, what would the post split market cap be?

6. Faye owned 1,300 shares of Wonderband Corp. Last week, a 2-for-1 split was executed. The pre-split price per share was w dollars.

   a. Determine the number of shares Faye owned after the split.

   b. Write an algebraic expression for the price per share after the split.

   c. Express the total value of the Wonderband stock Faye owned algebraically after the split.

7. Suppose that before a stock split, a share was selling for x dollars. After the stock split, the price was $\frac{2x}{3}$ dollars per share. What was the stock split ratio?

8. On December 14, XTO Energy Inc. executed a 5-for-4 split. At that time, Ed owned 553 shares of that stock. The price per share was $55.60 before the split. After the split, he received a check for a fractional part of a share. What was the amount of that check?

9. Yesterday, Tenser Inc. executed a 2-for-1 split. Jamie was holding 500 shares of the stock before the split and each was worth $34.12.

    a. What was the total value of her shares before the split?

    b. How many shares did she hold after the split?

    c. What was the post-split price per share?

    d. What was the total value of Jamie's shares after the split?

10. On May 30, Universe Inc. announced a 5-for-2 stock split. Before the split, the corporation had 340 million shares outstanding with a market value of $73.25 per share.

    a. How many shares were outstanding after the split?

    b. What was the post-split price per share?

    c. Show that this split was a "monetary non-event" for the corporation.

11. Two days ago, Lisa owned y shares of Postaero. Yesterday, the corporation instituted a 3-for-2 stock split. Before the split, each share was worth x dollars.

    a. How many shares did she hold after the split? Express your answer algebraically.

    b. What was the price per share after the split? Express your answer algebraically.

    c. Show that the split was a "monetary non-event" for Lisa.

12. Last week, Donna owned x shares of Spoonaire stock. Yesterday, the company instituted a 2-for-5 reverse split. The pre-split price per share was $3.40. The number of shares outstanding before the split was y.

    a. How many shares did Donna hold after the split? What was the post-split price per share?

    b. What was the post-split number of outstanding shares? What was the post-split market cap?

13. After a 5-for-2 stock split, Laura owned x shares of Skroyco stock. Each share was worth $16 after the split. What was the value of one share before the split?

8-9 Dividend Income

Exercises

1. Jared is purchasing a stock that pays an annual dividend of $3.42 per share.

   a. If he purchases 400 shares for $53.18 per share, what would his annual income be from dividends?

   b. What is the yield, to the nearest tenth of a percent?

2. Marianne purchased s shares of a corporation that pays a d dollars quarterly dividend per share. What is her annual dividend income, expressed algebraically?

3. Adrianna owns 1,000 shares of a corporation that pays an annual dividend of $2.17 per share. How much should she expect to receive on a quarterly dividend check?

4. Mr. Fierro owns x shares of stock. The annual dividend per share is q dollars. Express Mr. Fierro's quarterly dividend amount algebraically.

5. The annual dividend per share of a certain stock is d dollars. The current price of the stock is x dollars per share. What is the percent yield of the stock, expressed algebraically?

6. You bought x shares of a stock for y dollars per share. The annual dividend per share is d. Express the percent yield algebraically.

7. Stock in the Sister Golden Hair Shampoo Company was selling for $44.64 per share, and it was paying a $2.08 annual dividend. It underwent a 2-for-1 split.

   a. What was the new price of one share after the split?

   b. If you owned 300 shares before the split, how many shares did you own after the split?

   c. What was the annual dividend per share after the split?

   d. What was the yield, to the nearest tenth of a percent, before the split?

   e. What was the yield, to the nearest tenth of a percent, after the split?

8. One share of West World stock pays an annual dividend of $1.50. Today West World closed at $26.50 with a net change of –3.50. What was the stock's yield at yesterday's closing price?

9. The stock in a real estate corporation was selling for $6 per share, with an annual dividend of $0.12. It underwent a 2-for-5 reverse split.

   a. What was the value of a share after the reverse split?

   b. What was the annual dividend after the reverse split?

   c. What was the yield after the reverse split?

10. One share of Liam Corp. stock pays an annual dividend of d dollars. Today Liam closed at c dollars with a net change of $+h$. Write an expression for the stock's yield at yesterday's close.

11. In the summer of 2016, Apple was paying a $0.57 annual dividend. What would you receive on a quarterly dividend check if you had x shares of Apple at that time? Express your answer algebraically.

12. A corporation was paying a $4.20 annual dividend. The stock underwent a 3-for-2 split. What is the new annual dividend per share?

13. If you received a dividend check for d dollars and your stock had a quarterly dividend of p dollars, express the number of shares you owned algebraically.

14. Complete the missing entries in the table below. Round all dollar amounts to the nearest cent, and round all percents to the nearest tenth of a percent.

Price per Share at Wednesday's Close	Dividend	Wednesday's Net Change	Tuesday's Closing Price	Tuesday's Yield	Wednesday's Yield
$23	$0.96	+1	a.	b.	c.
$54.10	$2	d.	$54.88	e.	f.
W	D	C	g.	h.	i.

15. Pat owned 2,500 shares of Speed King Corporation, and received a quarterly dividend check for $925. What was the annual dividend for one share of Speed King?

16. Janet owned 114 shares of a corporation, and received a quarterly dividend check for y dollars. Express the annual dividend for one share algebraically.

17. A stock's dividend is not changing, yet its yield has fallen over the past five consecutive days. What had happened to the price of the stock over those last five days?

18. A stock's dividend was decreased on Tuesday. Does that mean its yield is lower on Tuesday than it was on Monday? Explain.

9-1 Innovations and Inventions

Exercises

1. Decide whether each of the following questions or statements are biased or not. (The random number table appears on page 145 and the normal curve table appears on page 146.)

    a. Do you think a person who doesn't vote is irresponsible?

    b. Do you agree or disagree with the fact that eating in class is not permitted?

    c. Don't you think Mr. Menchel should let us use calculators more often?

    d. How would you describe Mr. Rogala's car?

    e. Do you feel that hockey is more exciting than tennis?

    f. Do you avoid fast-food restaurants as part of a healthy diet?

2. A cosmetics company is deciding whether or not to modify a lipstick product they manufacture. They need to do some research. They want to test if women react differently to medicated lipsticks. They randomly select 500 women and randomly assign them to two different groups. One uses the medicated lipstick and the other uses non-medicated lipstick. Is this an example of an observational study or an experimental study?

3. A music school needs to test some new music stand designs, and they need to select 100 students randomly from an enrollment of 719 students.

    a. If they use the random number table, how many digits will they need to use to represent the students?

    b. If they use the random number table and start on line 10, what are the numbers of the first five students who will be selected?

4. A random group of 90 gas stations, from the 121,000 gas stations in the United States, is to be taken using the random number table.

    a. How many digits will be needed to be assigned to each gas station?

    b. Would it be possible for the random sample of 90 gas stations to contain only California gas stations?

    c. Would it be probable for the random sample of 90 gas stations to be all from California?

    d. Would it be possible for the random sample of 90 gas stations to be all the same brand?

    e. Would it be probable for the random sample of 90 gas stations to be the same brand?

Name _____   Date _____

5. A pharmaceutical company is testing a new drug to see if its effectiveness on lowering blood pressure is superior to the old drug. They randomly select 2,000 people and split them into two groups. One group takes the old drug and the other group takes the new medication. Is this an example of an observational study or an experiment?

6. The Plastico Plastics Company wants to test if its new cell phone screen protector is more resistant to scratches for a longer period of time than the current type of screen protector they manufacture. They will test 100 old covers and 100 new covers.

    a. Draw a diagram for a completely randomized design that describes the experiment.

    b. The life of the old protector is normally distributed with mean 42 months and standard deviation 3 months. The average life of the new protector was 52 months with a standard deviation of 2 months. Explain if you think the new protector is superior.

    c. If the new protector from part b had an average life of 43 months, would you believe the new protector is superior? Explain.

7. The Forever Tread Tire Company manufactures bicycle tires. They have developed a new type of tire that they plan to test on 200 customers' bicycles, randomly selected from their list of 8,476 customers.

    a. If they start on line 18 of the random number table, what will be the numbers of the first three customers selected?

    b. Why will a matched-pairs design be better than a completely randomized design for this study?

8. A holiday tree farm has developed a soil additive they think will make their trees grow faster, and taller. They need to conduct an experiment. They need to plant trees randomly into different containers—some with the soil additive and some without.

    a. Does a random assignment of trees guarantee that all the naturally heartier trees will not all be tested with the soil additive?

    b. Is it probable that all the heartier seeds will be placed with only the soil additive?

    c. If the test is conducted and the trees treated with the new fertilizer do in fact grow taller, and faster, would the company believe the soil additive worked as intended or that all the better, heartier trees happened to be, by chance, assigned to the new fertilizer containers?

9. The Power-Sure Battery Company designed a new type of long-lasting battery and they are testing it so they can set up an advertising campaign. They are going to pick 80 batteries from the first lot of 900 batteries to see if the batteries will last as many hours as they claim.

    a. If they number the batteries 001–900 and start at line 3 on the random number table, what are the numbers of the first five batteries that will be tested for defects?

    b. If the lifetime of the new batteries in a flashlight is normally distributed with mean 110 hours and standard deviation 10 hours, and they guarantee that their batteries will last at least 100 hours, what percent of the batteries will not meet that standard?

TABLE 1   Random Numbers

Row																				
1	4	5	1	8	5	0	3	3	7	1	2	8	4	5	1	1	0	9	5	7
2	4	2	2	5	8	0	4	5	7	0	7	0	3	6	6	1	3	1	3	1
3	8	9	9	3	4	3	5	0	6	3	9	1	1	8	2	6	9	2	0	9
4	8	9	0	7	2	9	9	0	4	7	6	7	4	7	1	3	4	3	5	3
5	5	7	3	1	0	3	7	4	7	8	5	2	0	1	3	7	7	6	3	6
6	0	9	3	8	7	6	7	9	9	5	6	2	5	6	5	8	4	2	6	4
7	4	1	0	1	0	2	2	0	4	7	5	1	1	9	4	7	9	7	5	1
8	6	4	7	3	6	3	4	5	1	2	3	1	1	8	0	0	4	8	2	0
9	8	0	2	8	7	9	3	8	4	0	4	2	0	8	9	1	2	3	3	2
10	9	4	6	0	6	9	7	8	8	2	5	2	9	6	0	1	4	6	0	5
11	6	6	9	5	7	4	4	6	3	2	0	6	0	8	9	1	3	6	1	8
12	0	7	1	7	7	7	2	9	7	8	7	5	8	8	6	9	8	4	1	0
13	6	1	3	0	9	7	3	3	6	6	0	4	1	8	3	2	6	7	6	8
14	2	2	3	6	2	1	3	0	2	2	6	6	9	7	0	2	1	2	5	8
15	0	7	1	7	4	2	0	0	0	1	3	1	2	0	4	7	8	4	1	0
16	6	6	5	1	6	1	8	1	5	5	2	6	2	0	1	1	5	2	3	6
17	9	9	6	2	5	3	5	9	8	3	7	5	0	1	3	9	3	8	0	8
18	9	9	9	6	1	2	9	3	4	6	5	6	4	6	5	8	2	7	4	0
19	2	5	6	3	1	9	8	1	1	0	3	5	6	7	9	1	4	5	2	0
20	5	1	1	9	8	1	2	1	1	6	9	8	1	8	1	9	9	1	2	0
21	1	9	8	0	7	4	6	8	4	0	3	0	8	1	1	0	6	2	3	2
22	9	7	0	9	6	3	8	9	9	7	0	6	5	4	3	6	5	0	3	2
23	1	7	6	4	8	2	0	3	9	6	3	6	2	1	0	7	7	3	1	7
24	6	2	5	8	2	0	7	8	6	4	6	6	8	9	2	0	6	9	0	4
25	1	5	7	1	1	1	9	5	1	4	5	2	8	3	4	3	0	7	3	5
26	1	4	6	6	5	6	0	1	9	4	0	5	2	7	6	4	3	6	8	8
27	1	8	5	0	2	1	6	8	0	7	7	2	6	2	6	7	5	4	8	7
28	7	8	7	4	6	5	4	3	7	9	3	9	2	7	9	5	4	2	3	1
29	1	6	3	2	8	3	7	3	0	7	2	4	8	0	9	9	9	4	7	0
30	2	8	9	0	8	1	6	8	1	7	3	1	3	0	9	7	2	5	7	9
31	0	7	8	8	6	5	7	5	5	4	0	0	3	4	1	2	7	3	7	9
32	8	4	0	1	4	5	1	9	1	1	2	1	5	3	2	8	5	5	7	5
33	7	3	5	9	7	0	4	9	1	2	1	3	2	5	1	9	3	3	8	3
34	4	7	2	6	7	6	9	9	2	7	8	7	5	5	5	2	4	4	3	4
35	9	3	3	7	0	7	0	5	7	5	6	9	5	4	3	1	4	6	6	8
36	0	2	4	9	7	8	1	6	3	8	7	8	0	5	6	7	2	7	5	0
37	7	1	0	1	8	4	7	1	2	9	3	8	0	0	8	7	9	2	8	6
38	9	7	9	4	4	5	3	1	9	3	4	5	0	6	3	5	9	6	9	8
39	0	4	2	5	0	0	9	9	6	4	0	6	9	0	3	8	3	5	7	2
40	0	7	1	2	3	6	1	7	9	3	9	5	4	6	8	4	8	8	0	6
41	3	5	6	6	2	4	4	5	6	3	7	8	7	6	5	2	0	4	3	2
42	6	6	8	5	5	2	9	7	9	3	3	1	6	9	5	9	7	1	1	2
43	9	5	0	4	3	1	1	7	3	9	2	7	7	4	7	0	3	1	2	8
44	5	1	7	8	9	4	2	2	9	2	8	9	9	8	0	6	3	7	2	1
45	1	6	3	9	4	1	3	2	1	1	8	5	6	3	4	1	9	3	1	7
46	4	4	8	6	4	0	3	8	3	8	3	5	9	5	9	4	8	3	9	4
47	7	7	6	6	4	5	4	4	8	4	4	0	3	9	8	5	2	0	2	3
48	2	5	6	6	3	7	0	6	5	6	9	0	1	9	5	2	6	9	1	2

Standard normal
probabilities (continued)

Tabulated area
=probability

Standard normal ( ) curve

0   z*

z*	.00	.01	.02	.03	.04	.05	.06	.07	.08	.09
0.0	.5000	.5040	.5080	.5120	.5160	.5199	.5239	.5279	.5319	.5359
0.1	.5398	.5438	.5478	.5517	.5557	.5596	.5636	.5675	.5714	.5753
0.2	.5793	.5832	.5871	.5910	.5948	.5987	.6026	.6064	.6103	.6141
0.3	.6179	.6217	.6255	.6293	.6331	.6368	.6406	.6443	.6480	.6517
0.4	.6554	.6591	.6628	.6664	.6700	.6736	.6772	.6808	.6844	.6879
0.5	.6915	.6950	.6985	.7019	.7054	.7088	.7123	.7157	.7190	.7224
0.6	.7257	.7291	.7324	.7357	.7389	.7422	.7454	.7486	.7517	.7549
0.7	.7580	.7611	.7642	.7673	.7704	.7734	.7764	.7794	.7823	.7852
0.8	.7881	.7910	.7939	.7967	.7995	.8023	.8051	.8078	.8106	.8133
0.9	.8159	.8186	.8212	.8238	.8264	.8289	.8315	.8340	.8365	.8389
1.0	.8413	.8438	.8461	.8485	.8508	.8531	.8554	.8577	.8599	.8621
1.1	.8643	.8665	.8686	.8708	.8729	.8749	.8770	.8790	.8810	.8830
1.2	.8849	.8869	.8888	.8907	.8925	.8944	.8962	.8980	.8997	.9015
1.3	.9032	.9049	.9066	.9082	.9099	.9115	.9131	.9147	.9162	.9177
1.4	.9192	.9207	.9222	.9236	.9251	.9265	.9279	.9292	.9306	.9319
1.5	.9332	.9345	.9357	.9370	.9382	.9394	.9406	.9418	.9429	.9441
1.6	.9452	.9463	.9474	.9484	.9495	.9505	.9515	.9525	.9535	.9545
1.7	.9554	.9564	.9573	.9582	.9591	.9599	.9608	.9616	.9625	.9633
1.8	.9641	.9649	.9656	.9664	.9671	.9678	.9686	.9693	.9699	.9706
1.9	.9713	.9719	.9726	.9732	.9738	.9744	.9750	.9756	.9761	.9767
2.0	.9772	.9778	.9783	.9788	.9793	.9798	.9803	.9808	.9812	.9817
2.1	.9821	.9826	.9830	.9834	.9838	.9842	.9846	.9850	.9854	.9857
2.2	.9861	.9864	.9868	.9871	.9875	.9878	.9881	.9884	.9887	.9890
2.3	.9893	.9896	.9898	.9901	.9904	.9906	.9909	.9911	.9913	.9916
2.4	.9918	.9920	.9922	.9925	.9927	.9929	.9931	.9932	.9934	.9936
2.5	.9938	.9940	.9941	.9943	.9945	.9946	.9948	.9949	.9951	.9952
2.6	.9953	.9955	.9956	.9957	.9959	.9960	.9961	.9962	.9963	.9964
2.7	.9965	.9966	.9967	.9968	.9969	.9970	.9971	.9972	.9973	.9974
2.8	.9974	.9975	.9976	.9977	.9977	.9978	.9979	.9979	.9980	.9981
2.9	.9981	.9982	.9982	.9983	.9984	.9984	.9985	.9985	.9986	.9986
3.0	.9987	.9987	.9987	.9988	.9988	.9989	.9989	.9989	.9990	.9990
3.1	.9990	.9991	.9991	.9991	.9992	.9992	.9992	.9992	.9993	.9993
3.2	.9993	.9993	.9994	.9994	.9994	.9994	.9994	.9995	.9995	.9995
3.3	.9995	.9995	.9995	.9996	.9996	.9996	.9996	.9996	.9996	.9997
3.4	.9997	.9997	.9997	.9997	.9997	.9997	.9997	.9997	.9997	.9998
3.5	.9998	.9998	.9998	.9998	.9998	.9998	.9998	.9998	.9998	.9998
3.6	.9998	.9998	.9999	.9999	.9999	.9999	.9999	.9999	.9999	.9999
3.7	.9999	.9999	.9999	.9999	.9999	.9999	.9999	.9999	.9999	.9999
3.8	.9999	.9999	.9999	.9999	.9999	.9999	.9999	.9999	.9999	1.0000

9-2 | Market Research

Exercises

1. Just Carpets has eight different quality grades of carpeting. Three types are being selected for a corporate test on durability.

   a. How many different samples of size 3 can be taken, without replacement?

   b. How many different samples of size 5 can be taken without replacement?

2. The Smithtown Highway Department is doing a survey on potholes and road conditions. They send a survey to all registered voters in their locale. Explain why this surveying technique is poor due to undercoverage.

3. As part of a quality control test on tennis racquets, Xander has to use a new racquet for 60 minutes each day for a month. Xander skips days, sometimes doesn't do the entire 60 minutes, and sometimes he plays for more than 60 minutes. Is this an example of undercoverage or nonresponse? Explain.

4. A sporting goods store sells 10 brands of golf clubs. Four will be randomly chosen to be put on sale this week. If one of the four must be the Golf King brand, how many different combinations of four can be put on sale?

5. A local YMCA is looking to get feedback on its swim program from the 200 people who are enrolled in swimming lessons. They are taking a stratified random sample of 50 swimming students because they want the sample to have the same percentage breakdown as the entire group of swimmers. The following table gives the percent breakdown of swim students at this YMCA:

   a. How many elementary aged students should be randomly selected for this survey?

   b. How many adults should be randomly selected for this survey?

Age Group	Percent
Elementary School	20%
Teenagers	32%
Adults	48%

   c. If the YMCA had taken a simple random sample, would have it been possible to have the sample be comprised solely of elementary school students? Explain.

6. The Bel Air Vintage Car Company manufactures replacement parts for old cars. A new machine that manufactures steering wheels produced the following number of defective wheels during the last five-day work week:

Monday (M) 7
Tuesday (U) 18
Wednesday (W) 21
Thursday (H) 31
Friday (F) 33

a. Find the range of the distribution of defects.

b. There are five different samples of size 4 possible. List the five possible samples using the letters M, U, W, H, F.

c. Find the range of each of the five samples found in part b.

d. Find the mean of the five sample ranges from part c.

e. Does the mean of the five sample ranges equal the original range you found in part a?

f. Is the range an unbiased estimator?

g. Find the mean of the original distribution of defects.

h. Is the mean an unbiased estimator?

i. Find the standard deviation σ of the original distribution. Round to the nearest hundredth.

7. The economics department of a local college is looking to determine the banking knowledge of their graduating seniors. Professor Klopfer has a class of seniors in his macroeconomics class and agrees to give the survey there. Explain why this survey is biased.

8. The Ticket to Read bookstore is planning to analyze the spending habits of college students. A professor of freshman physics volunteers to have his class take the survey.

a. What type of sample is this?

b. Can you give a disadvantage of surveying this way?

c. Is limiting the survey to freshman is an example of undercoverage or nonresponse?

9. A local Honda dealer is looking to determine the public's opinion on foreign versus domestic automobiles. They send a survey to all of their customers. Explain why this survey is biased.

10. The Fit It Fast tool company is planning to address a recent problem with theft of tools. The management is doing a survey of random employees. They randomly select 100 employees and have them fill out an anonymous questionnaire. Which do you think is a greater problem in this scenario, nonresponse or undercoverage? Explain.

11. Lawnmasters Landscaping is planning a marketing strategy for the upcoming year. They plan on doing on survey to see how many residents in their neighborhoods mow their own lawns. They have their secretaries randomly call home weekdays during their 9am–5pm work shift, and find out that only 17% of the homeowners mow their own lawns. Do you think this is an overestimate, underestimate, or good approximation of the actual population percent of people who mow their own lawns? Explain.

12. The local tax assessor of Peconic County is seeking information on requiring taxpayers to pay their taxes electronically instead of with checks in the mail. They send a survey to all residents who served jury duty within the past two years in their locale. Explain why this surveying technique is poor.

9-3 Supply and Demand

Exercises

1. Wayne's Widget World sells widgets to stores for $9.20 each. A local store marks them up $8.79. What is the retail price at this store?

2. The wholesale price of an item is *w* dollars. The retail price is *p* percent higher. Express the retail price algebraically.

3. The Knockey Corporation sells hockey sticks at a wholesale price of $103. If a store marks this up 106%, what is the retail price?

4. A tire company sells bicycle tires to retailers for *t* dollars. The Mineola Bike Shop marks them up 80%. Express the retail price at the Mineola Bike Shop algebraically.

5. The following graph shows the supply and demand curves for a widget.

   a. Explain what will happen if the price is set at $9.

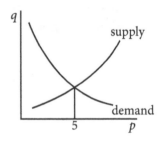

   b. Use the graph above to explain what will happen if the price is set at $2.75.

6. An automobile DVD/navigation system sells to stores at a wholesale price of $497. A popular national chain store sells them for $879.99. What is the markup?

7. A guitar sells for a retail price of *g* dollars. The wholesale price of the guitar is *w*. Write an expression for the markup and an expression for the percent of the markup.

8. An automobile ski rack is sold to stores at a wholesale price of $38. If a store has a $23 markup, what is the retail price of the ski rack? Find the percent of the markup, to the nearest percent.

9. A manufacturer takes a poll of several retailers to determine how many widgets they would buy at different wholesale prices. The results are shown. What is the equation of the demand function? Round values to the nearest hundredth. Use the demand function to determine how many widgets, to the nearest hundred, retailers would buy at a price of $20.

Wholesale Price	23	26	28	30	33	35	37	40
Quantities Retailers Will Purchase (1,000s)	4,000	3,450	3,100	2,550	2,000	1,900	1,750	1,400

10. The graph shows supply and demand curves for the AquaPod, a digital music player for scuba divers.

    a. What is the equilibrium price?

    b. What will happen if the price is set at $35?

    c. How many AquaPods are demanded at a price of $35?

    d. How many AquaPods are supplied at a price of $40?

    e. What will happen if the price is set at $45?

11. The Greencup Company produces paper cups. They have developed a new type of insulated cup that is biodegradable and doesn't allow the cup to get too hot to hold. They want to use the demand function to help them set a price. They survey dozens of retailers to get an approximation of how many cups would be demanded at each price.

Wholesale Price p (pack of 50)	$5	$5.50	$6	$6.50	$7	$7.50	$8	$8.50	$9	$9.50
Quantity, q (1,000s)	5,100	4,900	4,600	4,200	3,700	2,400	2,100	1,600	700	200

    a. Find the equation of the linear regression line. Round to the nearest thousandth.

    b. Give the slope of the regression line and give an interpretation of its units.

    c. Find the correlation coefficient and interpret the value. Round to the nearest thousandth.

    d. Based on the regression line, how many packages of cups would be demanded at a wholesale price of $4? Round to the nearest hundred.

    e. Was your answer to part d an example of extrapolation or interpolation? Explain.

    f. If the company sold 5,100,000 packages of cups at a price of $5 each, how much money would they take in?

    g. If the company sold 200,000 packages of cups at a price of $9.50 each, how much money would they take in?

    h. Compare your answers to parts f and g. Why is it not correct to conclude that more profit is made by selling for $5 than for $9.50?

9-4 Fixed and Variable Expenses

Exercises

1. The fixed expenses for producing widgets are $947,900. The labor and materials required for each widget produced costs $16.44. Represent the total expenses as a function of the quantity q produced.

2. A widget manufacturer's expense equation is $E = 14q + 29,000$. What are the variable costs to produce one widget?

3. The Catania Cat Corporation manufactures litter boxes for cats. Their expense function is $E = 4.18q + 82,000$. Find the average cost of producing 10,000 litter boxes.

4. The expense function for a certain item is $E = 2.95q + 712,000$. Express the average cost of producing q items algebraically.

5. The Mizzi Corporation has created a demand function for one of its wrench sets. It expresses the quantity demanded in terms of the wholesale price p, and it was created by surveying retailers and using linear regression. The demand function is $q = -98p + 5,788$. Their expense function is $E = 23q + 68,000$. Express the expense function as a function in terms of p.

6. A corporation's expense function is $E = 7.50q + 34,000$. The demand function was determined to be $q = -5.5p + 6,000$. Express the expense function in terms of the price.

7. Wexler's manufactures widgets. They create a monthly expense equation of all expenses in one month of manufacturing. The expense equation is $E = 2.10q + 7,600$. They plan to sell the widgets to retailers at a wholesale price of $3.50 each.

    a. How many widgets must be sold so that the income from the widgets is equal to the expense of producing them? Round to the nearest widget.

    b. If the company sells 2,900 widgets, how much money will they lose?

8. Find the breakeven point for the expense equation $E = 6.25q + 259,325$ and the revenue function $R = 12q$.

9. The NFW Corporation produces a product with fixed expenses of f dollars and variable expenses of v dollars per item. If q represents quantity produced, write the expense function.

10. The Burden Corporation manufactures racquets. The racquets have the expense equation $E = rq + f$. What is the average cost of producing x racquets?

11. The DiMonte Corporation invented a new type of sunglass lens. Their variable expenses are $12.66 per unit, and their fixed expenses are $111,200.

   a. How much does it cost them to produce one lens? 15,000 lenses?

   b. Express the expense function algebraically. What is the slope of the expense function?

   c. If the slope is interpreted as a rate, give the units to use.

   d. What is the average cost, to the nearest cent, of producing 15,000 lenses?

   e. What is the average cost, to the nearest cent, of producing 17,000 lenses?

   f. As the number of lenses increased from 15,000 to 17,000, did the average expense per lens increase or decrease?

12. The expense equation for a new business venture is $E = 4.55q + 28,500$. If the owners have $100,000 to start up this operation, what quantity can they produce initially if they spend all of this money on production? Round to the nearest hundred units.

13. The graph shows Expense (E) and Revenue (R) functions and several different levels of quantity produced.

   a. What are the coordinates of the breakeven point?

   b. If U units are produced, will there be a profit or a loss?

   c. Compare the profit made if W units are produced to the profit made if T units are produced. Which level of production yields a greater profit? How can you tell?

14. The fixed costs of producing a Winner Widget are f dollars. The variable costs are v dollars per widget. If the average cost of producing q Winner Widgets is a, express the fixed cost f in terms of a, v, and q.

15. Explain why the y-intercept of the expense function is never 0, while the y-intercept of the revenue function is always 0.

9-5 Graphs of Expense and Revenue Functions

Exercises

1. Examine the graphs of an expense function and a revenue function.

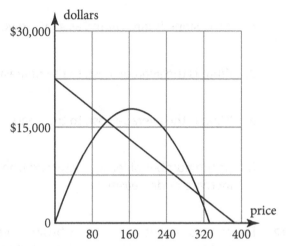

   a. What is the price at which the maximum revenue is attained?

   b. Estimate the maximum revenue.

   c. Estimate the leftmost breakeven point.

   d. Estimate the rightmost breakeven point.

2. Identify the maximum point by using the axis of symmetry.

   a. $R = -2{,}000p^2 + 44{,}000p$

   b. $R = -125p^2 + 3{,}200p$

3. Geoff's company manufactures customized T-shirts. Each shirt costs $2.00 to manufacture and print. The fixed costs for this product line are $2,000. The demand function is $q = -1{,}200p + 7{,}800$, where p is the price for each shirt.

   a. Write the expense equation in terms of the demand q.

   b. Express the expense equation from part a in terms of the price p.

   c. Write the revenue function in terms of the price.

   d. Graph the functions in an appropriate viewing window. What price yields the maximum revenue? What is the revenue at that price? Identify the price at the breakeven points. Round answers to the nearest cent.

   e. Use any of the methods you learned in this section to determine the roots of the revenue equation. Interpret those roots in the context of this problem.

4. Mobile Tech manufactures cell phone accessories. A particular item in their product line costs $40 each to manufacture. The fixed costs are $120,000. The demand function is $q = -120p + 8,000$, where q is the quantity the public will buy given the price p.

a. Write the expense function in terms of p.

b. Identity an appropriate viewing window for the domain of the expense function.

c. Construct the graph of the expense function from part a.

d. What is the revenue equation for this Mobile Tech product? Write the revenue equation in terms of the price.

e. Use the revenue equation from part d. What would the revenue be if the price of the item was set at $60?

f. Use any of the methods you learned in this section to determine the roots of the revenue equation. Interpret those roots in the context of this problem.

g. Graph the revenue function found in part d.

h. Which price would yield the higher revenue, $20 or $40?

i. Graph the expense and revenue functions found above. Interpret the graph.

9-6 Breakeven Analysis

Exercises

1. AVS Industries has determined that the combined fixed and variable expenses for the production and sale of 800,000 items are $24,000,000. What is the price at the breakeven point for this item?

2. The expense equation for the production of a certain audio player is $E = 1{,}250q + 700{,}000$, where q is the quantity demanded. At a particular price, the breakeven revenue is $3,800,000. What is the quantity demanded at the breakeven point?

3. A manufacturer determines that a product will reach the breakeven point if sold at either $30 or $120. At $30, the expense and revenue values are both $120,000. At $120, the expense and revenue values are both $400,000. Graph possible revenue and expense functions that would depict this situation. Label the maximum and minimum values for each of the axes. Circle the breakeven points.

4. Estimate the breakeven points of the expense and revenue functions in each graph.

a.

b.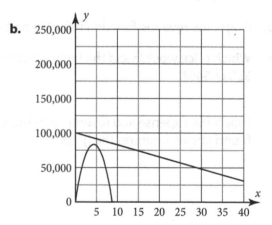

5. Sound Foundations Inc. is a firm that manufactures concrete building supplies. Their research department has invented a new product that they want to sell to builders. After extensive analysis, they have found that their breakeven point will occur only once when the price of the item is $1,200. At this price, the expense and revenue will be $3,500,000. Graph possible revenue and expense functions that would depict this situation. Label the maximum and minimum values for each of the axes. Circle the breakeven point and interpret the graph.

6. Sunset Park Equipment produces camping gear. They are considering manufacturing a new energy-efficient lantern. The expense function is $E = -54{,}000p + 7{,}000{,}000$ and the revenue function is $R = -1{,}800p^2 + 200{,}000p$.

   a. Sketch the graphs of the expense and revenue functions.

   b. Determine the prices at the breakeven points. Round to the nearest cent.

   c. Use your answers from part b to determine the revenue and expense amounts for each of the breakeven points. Round to the nearest cent.

7. Baby-B-Good manufactures affordable plastic baby rattles. The expense equation is $E = -3{,}400p + 50{,}000$, and the revenue equation is $R = -1{,}800p^2 + 20{,}000p$.

   a. Sketch the graph of the expense and revenue functions.

   b. Determine the prices at the breakeven points. Round to the nearest cent.

   c. Use your answers from part b to determine the revenue and expense amounts for each of the breakeven points. Round to the nearest cent.

8. Approximate both the expense and revenue functions shown in the graph in terms of price x.

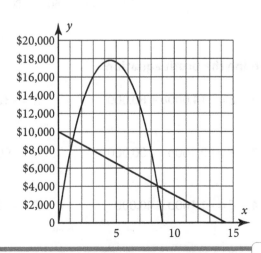

9-7 | The Profit Equation

Exercises

1. Maximum profit can be found on the graph where the difference between the revenue and expense functions is the greatest. Examine each of the following graphs and estimate the maximum profit price and the maximum profit at that price.

a.

b.

c.

d.
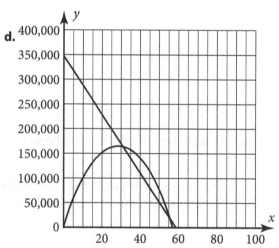

Determine the profit equation.

2. $E = -14{,}000p + 80{,}000$ $R = -32{,}200p^2 + 106{,}000p$

3. $E = -2{,}100p + 100{,}000$ $R = -900p^2 + 20{,}000p$

4. $E = -1{,}100p + 40{,}000$ $R = -150p^2 + 3{,}800p$

5. The expense and revenue function can yield a profit function. That equation can represent no profit made for any price.

   a. Use your graphing calculator and the revenue equation from Exercise 2 to determine an expense equation that would yield a situation where no profit can be made.

   b. Use your graphing calculator and the expense equation from Exercise 3 to determine a revenue equation that would yield a situation where no profit can be made.

6. Determine the maximum profit and the price that would yield the maximum profit for each equation.

   a. $P = -500p^2 + 67,600p - 20,000$ b. $P = -370p^2 + 8,800p - 25,000$

   c. $P = -31p^2 + 4,540p - 9,251$

7. Listen Up sells external computer speakers. Their new product has the following expense and revenue functions: $E = -828p + 400,000$ and $R = -38p^2 + 8,000p$.

   a. Determine the profit function.

   b. Determine the price, to the nearest cent, which yields the maximum profit.

   c. Determine the maximum profit to the nearest cent.

8. FunFleece Incorporated manufactures fleece hats. It is considering making a new type of weatherproof fleece hat. The expense and revenue functions are $E = -300p + 150,000$ and $R = -300p^2 + 29,000p$.

   a. Determine the profit function.

   b. Determine the price, to the nearest cent, which yields the maximum profit.

   c. Determine the maximum profit to the nearest cent.

9. Determine the expense equation given the profit and revenue equations.
   $P = -468p^2 + 45,599p - 299,000$ $R = -468p^2 + 45,000p$

10. Determine the revenue equation given the profit and expense equations.
    $P = -525p^2 + 65,326p - 185,000$ $E = -326p + 185,000$

11. Hi-Res Industries is a new company with a single product in production. They calculate their profit equation to be $P = -150p^2 + 30,000p - 2,343,750$.

Determine the price values where the profit is equal to zero and the price at which the profit is a maximum.

9-8 Mathematically Modeling a Business

Exercises

Use the graph of the expense function (Y_1), the revenue function (Y_2), and the profit function (Y_3) to answer Exercises 1–3.

1. Name the coordinates of the maximum revenue point.

2. Name the coordinates of the maximum profit point.

3. What is the significance of the point (F, C)?

You are the CEO of Widget World Corporation. Researchers have developed a new electronic widget. The fixed costs to make the widget will be $30,000, and the variable cost will be $150 per widget. Exercises 4–13 are about the Widget World Corporation.

4. Write the expense function for the electronic widget in terms of q where q is the quantity that will be produced.

5. The market research department conducted consumer surveys and reported the following results. In these ordered pairs, the first number represents the **possible price** and the second number represents the **quantity demanded.** The points are listed as (p, q).

   (75, 6500), (100, 5900), (125, 4500), (150, 3900), (175, 2800), (200, 1500), (225, 900)

   You now need to set up a demand function using the ordered pairs from the market research department. Enter these ordered pairs into graphing calculator lists. Write the linear regression equation that models this set of ordered pairs. Round each coefficient to the nearest integer.

6. The equations used are in terms of q and p. Replace y with q and replace x with p. Write the new equation for q in terms of p.

7. Recall that the revenue equation is $R = pq$. Substitute the quantity (demand) equation from Exercise 6 into the revenue equation and simplify.

8. Use the equation for the demand from Exercise 6. Substitute this into your expense equation from Exercise 4 to write an expense equation in terms of p rather than q.

9. Enter the equation for *R* as Y_1 and the equation for *E* as Y_2 in your graphing calculator. What viewing window will you use to graph Y_1 and Y_2 in the same window?

10. Make a sketch of the graphs.

11. Find the coordinates of the breakeven points in your graph in Exercise 10. Round the coordinates to the nearest whole number.

12. Write the profit equation in terms of *x* (the price variable) by subtracting the expense equation from the revenue equation. Let Y_3 represent the profit. What will you enter in your calculator?

13. Enter the profit equation into your graphing calculator and determine the maximum profit price and amount to the nearest integer.

a. The *x*-value represents the price at which each widget should be set in order to get maximum profit. What is that price?

b. The *y*-value represents the maximum profit. What is that profit?

9-9 | Optimal Outcomes

Exercises

1. Determine whether each of the following points falls within the profit feasible region defined by $x \geq 0, y \geq 0, 7x + 3y \leq 45$.

   a. (2, 2) **b.** (5, 1) **c.** (6, 4)

   d. (4, 8) **e.** (0, 15)

2. The vertices of a feasible region are listed below. What is the maximum profit for the objective equation $P = 120x + 170y$

   a. (0,300), (0,0), (1200,0)

   b. (20,70), (60,80), (80,90), (40,10)

3. The vertices of a feasible region are listed below. What is the minimum cost for the objective equation $C = 57x + 88y$

   a. (2,9), (10,20), (15,13), (8,2)

   b. (50,80), (70,120), (90,180), (120,90)

4. In each of the following, you are given an objective function and the vertices of a feasible region. Determine both the maximum and minimum values of the objective function as well as the point at which they occur.

   a. $P = 81x + 57y$ (6, 3), (10, 10), (15, 7)

   b. $C = 98.15x + 63.5y$ (0, 800), (40, 1000), (100, 900), (60, 200), (50, 50)

5. Circuitry Inc. produces two types of circuit boards. Their profits are $400 for Circuit 1 and $300 for Circuit 2. The process involves both types of circuits to be manufactured on both machine A and machine B. It takes 2 hours on machine A and 1.5 hours on machine B to manufacture Circuit 1. It takes 1 hour on machine A and 1.5 hours on machine B to manufacture Circuit 2. Because the company produces other electronics, they can allocate no more than 100 hours per day for circuit production on machine A and no more than 90 hours a day for circuit production on machine B. Let x represent the number of Circuit 1s produced and y represent the number of Circuit 2s produced.

   a. Write the profit objective function.

   b. Write the machine A constraint inequality.

   c. Write the machine B constraint inequality.

   d. Graph the constraint inequalities. Identify the coordinates of the feasible region.

   e. How many of each type of circuits must they sell to maximize their profits?

6. A financial manager wants to invest up to $600,000 of his client's money in two investment plans. The Focused Plan pays an annual interest rate of 4% and the Strategic Plan pays an annual interest rate of 7%. The manager feels that in order to get the best return, the client should invest no less than $150,000 in the Focused Plan and no less than $250,000 in the Strategic Plan. How much should be invested in each plan to maximize the return?

   a. Let x represent the amount invested in the Focused Plan. Write an expression for the interest received from this investment.

   b. Let y represent the amount invested in the Strategic Plan. Write an expression for the interest received from this investment.

   c. Use parts a and b to write the return (R) objective function.

   d. Write the constraint that represents the limit on the total amount that can be invested. This will be one of the constraints that form the feasible region.

   e. Write an inequality that represents the suggested amount to be invested in the Focused Plan.

   f. Write an inequality that represents the suggested amount to be invested in the Strategic Plan.

   g. Graph the feasible region.

   h. Determine the vertices of the feasible region.

   i. Which vertex of the feasible region will maximize the return on the investment? What is that maximum return?

7. Liam Anthony is a financial advisor. He wants to invest up to $250,000 of his client's money in two investment plans. The Apex Plan pays an annual interest rate of 5% and the Multi- Plan pays an annual interest rate of 6%. Although the Multi-Plan pays a higher interest rate, there is some risk involved. Liam and the client have agreed to invest at most 50% of the total in the Multi-Plan. Liam feels that in order to get the best return, the client should invest no less than $100,000. How much should be invested in each plan to maximize the return?

a. Let x represent the amount invested in the Apex Plan. Write an expression for the interest received from this investment.

b. Let y represent the amount invested in the Multi-Plan. Write an expression for the interest received from this investment.

c. Use parts a and b to write the return objective function.

d. Write the constraint that represents the limit on the total amount that can be invested. This will be one of the constraints that form the feasible region.

e. Write an expression that represents the total amount that can be invested.

f. Write an expression that represents 50% of the total amount found in part e.

g. Liam is recommending that the amount invested in the Multi-Plan be no more than the amount found in part f. Write this inequality.

h. Use the distributive property to simplify the inequality found in g.

i. Combine like terms. Simplify the inequality. This will be one of the constraints that form the feasible region.

j. Write the inequality representing the manager's recommendation for the total amount that should be invested. This will be one of the constraints that form the feasible region.

k. Graph the feasible region.

l. Determine the vertices of the feasible region.

m. Which vertex of the feasible region will maximize the return on the investment? What is that maximum return?

8. Extreme Climb makes camping fabric that is a mixture of polyester and nylon. Their warehouse has 6000 lots of polyester and 3000 lots of nylon available during the week of June 1 for production of their Peak Performance and Rugged Performance fabrics. A roll of Peak Performance fabric uses 80 lots of polyester and 30 lots of nylon. A roll of Rugged Performance uses 40 lots of polyester and 30 lots of nylon. They make a profit of $90 per roll on the Peak Performance and $150 per roll on the Rugged Performance. How many rolls of each type should they manufacture during this week to maximize profit?

9. Industry City is a start-up company that produces picnic table sets made from recycled metal. Right now, Industry City has two big clients—River Cottages and Oceanside Resorts. River Cottages needs at least 60 tables, and Oceanside Resorts needs at most 150 tables. Industry City is able to produce and send at most 400 tables to these two clients. It cost $80 per table to ship to River Cottages, and $60 per table to ship to Oceanside Resorts. In return for the purchases, River Cottages has agreed to give Industry City $20 in rebates for each table purchased. Oceanside gives $30 in rebates toward for each table purchased. The owner of Industry City has determined that the company needs at least $2400 in credits to keep shipping costs down. How many tables should be shipped to American and Oceanside to minimize shipping costs? What is the minimum cost?

   a. Let x represent the number of tables shipped to River Cottages and y represent the number of tables shipped to Oceanside Resorts. Set up the cost objective function.

   b. Write the River Cottages constraint inequality for the number of tables needed.

   c. Write the Oceanside Resorts constraint inequality for the number of tables needed.

   d. Write the constraint inequality for the total number of tables Industry City is able to ship to these two locations.

   e. Write the constraint inequality for the credits.

   f. Graph the feasible region.

   g. Identify the vertices.

   h. What values will minimize cost in the objective function?

10. Raul and Carla own The Cakery Bakery. They make specialty cakes for all occasions. They have just been hired to provide the desserts for a large convention that will be held in one week. They will need to hire bakers and cake decorators. Bakers make $600 per week and cake decorators $900 per week. The company knows that they will need at least 3 bakers and at least 5 cake decorators. A baker spends 4 hours designing and 15 hours creating the cakes. A cake decorator spends 8 hours designing and 15 hours creating the cakes. Raul and Carla know that they will need at least 80 hours of design and 180 hours of creation. How many bakers and decorators will be needed for this job in order to keep costs at a minimum?

a. Let x represent the number of bakers needed and y represent the number of decorators needed. Write the cost objective function.

b. Write the constraint inequality for the number of bakers needed for this job.

c. Write the constraint inequality for the number of decorators needed for this job.

d. Complete the following table.

	Design	Creation
Baker	____ hours	____ hours
Decorator	____ hours	____ hours

e. Use your table to write the constraint inequality for the design hours needed to complete this job.

f. Use your table to write the constraint inequality for the creation hours needed to complete this job.

g. Graph the feasible region. You will notice that it is not a closed polygon. Rather, this is a boundless region because there is no upper constraint to form the polygon. Because you will be looking to minimize the cost objective function, this will not be a problem.

h. Identify the vertices of the feasible region.

i. Use the vertices and the cost objective function to determine the number of bakers and the number of decorators who must be hired for the job to minimize cost.

10-1 Retirement Income from Savings

Exercises

1. Ethan is 48 years old. He is planning on retiring when he turns 62. He has opened an IRA with an APR of 2.95% compounded monthly. If he makes monthly deposits of $850 to the account, how much will he have in the account when he is ready to retire?

2. Conor is 21 years old and just started working after college. He has opened a retirement account that pays 2.5% interest compounded monthly. He plans on making monthly deposits of $200. How much will he have in the account when he reaches $59\frac{1}{2}$ years of age?

3. Carla opened a retirement account that pays P percent interest compounded monthly. If she has direct deposits of X dollars per month taken out of her paycheck, write an expression that represents her balance after Y years.

4. Gillian started a retirement account with $10,000 when she turned 35. The account compounds interest quarterly at a rate of 3.625%. She made no further deposits into the account. After 20 years, she decided to withdraw 40% of what had accumulated in the account so that she could make her home handicap accessible. She had to pay a 10% penalty on the early withdrawal. What was her penalty?

5. Tanya is 42 years old. She would like to open a retirement account so that she will have one-half million dollars in the account when she retires at the age of 65. How much must she deposit each month into an account with an APR of 2.75% compounded monthly in order to reach her goal?

6. John is $59\frac{1}{2}$ years old. He plans to retire in 3 years. He now has $600,000 in a savings account that yields 3.4% interest compounded continuously. He has calculated that his final working year's salary will be $115,000. He has been told by his financial advisor that he should have 60% to 70% of his final year annual income available for use each year when he is retired.

   a. What is the range of income that his financial advisor feels he must have per year after he retires?

   b. Use the continuous compounding formula to determine how much he will have in his account at the beginning of retirement.

   c. If he uses 60% of his final annual salary, not accounting for any interest accrued in the account, how many years will he be able to tap into this account in his retirement?

7. Melanie has been contributing to a retirement account that pays 3.875% interest with pretax dollars. This account compounds interest monthly. She has put $300 per month into the account. At the end of 8 years, she needed money for a down payment on a new home. She withdrew 25% of the money that was in the account.

   a. Rounded to the nearest dollar, how much did she withdraw?

   b. Because she is in the 21% tax bracket, what was her tax liability on the amount of the withdrawal (rounded to the nearest dollar)?

   c. She had to pay a 10% early withdrawal penalty. How much was she required to pay (rounded to the nearest dollar)?

   d. How much did this withdrawal "cost" her?

8. Van is an office supervisor who has been contributing to his retirement account for the last Y years with pre-tax dollars. The account compounds interest quarterly at a rate of P percent. He contributes D dollars into the account after each 3-month period and this has not changed over the life of the account.

   a. Write an expression to represent the balance in the account after Y years of saving.

   b. After M years of contributions (where M is greater than Y), he needed to withdraw W percent of the money in his account. Write an expression for the withdrawal amount.

   c. Van pays T percent of his income in taxes. Write an algebraic expression for the combined total of his tax liability and the 10% early withdrawal penalty.

9. Meryl contributed 500 pre-tax dollars per month into her retirement account last tax year. Her taxable income for the year was $77,480. She files taxes as a married filing separately taxpayer.

    a. What would her taxable income have been had she contributed to the account in after-tax dollars?

    b. Use the tax table below to calculate her tax liability in both the pre-tax and after-tax contribution situation

    c. How much did Meryl save in taxes during that year?

If line 27 (taxable income) is—		And you are —			
At least	But less than	Single	Married filing jointly *	Married filing separately	Head of a household
		Your tax is —			
77,000					
77,000	77,050	15,050	10,844	15,093	13,579
77,050	77,100	15,063	10,856	15,107	13,591
77,100	77,150	15,075	10,869	15,127	13,604
77,150	77,200	15,088	10,881	15,135	13,616
77,200	77,250	15,100	10,894	15,149	13,629
77,250	77,300	15,113	10,906	15,163	13,641
77,300	77,350	15,125	10,919	15,177	13,654
77,350	77,400	15,138	10,931	15,191	13,666
77,400	77,450	15,150	10,944	15,205	13,679
77,450	77,500	15,163	10,956	15,219	13,691
77,500	77,550	15,175	10,969	15,233	13,704
77,550	77,600	15,188	10,981	15,247	13,716
77,600	77,650	15,200	10,994	15,261	13,729
77,650	77,700	15,213	11,006	15,275	13,741
77,700	77,750	15,225	11,019	15,289	13,754
77,750	77,800	15,238	11,031	15,303	13,766
77,800	77,850	15,250	11,044	15,317	13,779
77,850	77,900	15,263	11,056	15,331	13,791
77,900	77,950	15,275	11,069	15,345	13,804
77,950	78,000	15,288	11,081	15,359	13,816

If line 27 (taxable income) is—		And you are —			
At least	But less than	Single	Married filing jointly *	Married filing separately	Head of a household
		Your tax is —			
80,000					
80,000	80,050	15,800	11,594	15,933	14,329
80,050	80,100	15,813	11,606	15,947	14,341
80,100	80,150	15,825	11,619	15,961	14,354
80,150	80,200	15,838	11,631	15,975	14,366
80,200	80,250	15,850	11,644	15,989	14,379
80,250	80,300	15,863	11,656	16,003	14,391
80,300	80,350	15,875	11,669	16,017	14,404
80,350	80,400	15,888	11,681	16,031	14,416
80,400	80,450	15,900	11,694	16,045	14,429
80,450	80,500	15,913	11,706	16,059	14,441
80,500	80,550	15,925	11,719	16,073	14,454
80,550	80,600	15,938	11,731	16,087	14,486
80,600	80,650	15,950	11,744	16,101	14,479
80,650	80,700	15,963	11,756	16,115	14,491
80,700	80,750	15,975	11,769	16,129	14,504
80,750	80,800	15,988	11,781	16,143	14,516
80,800	80,850	16,000	11,794	16,157	14,529
80,850	80,900	16,013	11,806	16,171	14,541
80,900	80,950	16,025	11,819	16,185	14,554
80,950	81,000	16,038	11,831	16,199	14,566

If line 27 (taxable income) is—		And you are —			
At least	But less than	Single	Married filing jointly*	Married filing separately	Head of a household
		Your tax is —			
83,000					
83,000	83,050	16,550	12,344	16,773	15,079
83,050	83,100	16,563	12,356	16,787	15,091
83,100	83,150	16,575	12,369	16,801	15,104
83,150	83,200	16,588	12,381	16,815	15,116
83,200	83,250	16,600	12,394	16,829	15,129
83,250	83,300	16,613	12,406	16,843	15,141
83,300	83,350	16,625	12,419	16,857	15,154
83,350	83,400	16,638	12,431	16,871	15,166
83,400	83,450	16,650	12,444	16,885	15,179
83,450	83,500	16,663	12,456	16,899	15,191
83,500	83,550	16,675	12,469	16,913	15,204
83,550	83,600	16,688	12,481	16,927	15,216
83,600	83,650	16,700	12,494	16,941	15,229
83,650	83,700	16,713	12,506	16,955	15,241
83,700	83,750	16,725	12,519	16,969	15,254
83,750	83,800	16,738	12,531	16,983	15,266
83,800	83,850	16,750	12,544	16,997	15,279
83,850	83,900	16,763	12,556	17,011	15,291
83,900	83,950	16,775	12,569	17,025	15,304
83,950	84,000	16,788	12,581	17,039	15,316

10. Pei is a 26-year-old television executive. She files taxes as a single taxpayer. She needed to withdraw $30,000 from her tax-deferred retirement account to assist her parents with some financial problems. Pei's gross taxable income for the year in question was $162,983.

Schedule X— If your filing status is **Single**

If your taxable income is:		The tax is:	of the amount over—
Over—	But not over—		
$0	$9,225	········· 10%	$0
9,225	37,450	$922.50 + 15%	9,225
37,450	90,750	5,156.25 + 25%	37,450
90,750	189,300	18,481.25 + 28%	90,750
189,300	411,500	46,075.25 + 33%	189,300
411,500	413,200	119,401.25 + 35%	411,500
413,200	·········	119,996.25 + 39.6%	413,200

   a. Use the tax schedule to calculate Pei's tax liability had she not made the early withdrawal.

   b. Use the same worksheet to calculate her liability with an increase in her taxable income of $30,000.

   c. How much more in taxes did she pay because of the early withdrawal?

   d. What was her early withdrawal penalty?

11. Annette makes $96,000 per year working for an online e-magazine. Her company offers a 401K retirement plan in which they will match 45% of her contributions to the 401K up to 9% of her salary. The company will only allow employees to make contributions to the 401K to a maximum of 25% of their salary. For the year in question, the maximum allowable contribution to any 401K is $22,000 because she is over the age of 55.

   a. What is the maximum Annette's employer will allow for her contribution?

   b. What is the maximum contribution she could make?

   c. What is her employer's maximum contribution amount?

10-2 | Social Security Benefits

Exercises

1. In 2016, the maximum taxable income for Social Security was $118,500 with a 6.2% tax rate.

    a. What is the maximum anyone could have paid into Social Security tax in the year 2016?

    b. Ravi had two jobs in 2016. One employer paid him $69,810 and the other paid him $61,200. Each employer took out 6.2% for Social Security. How much did Ravi overpay in Social Security for 2016?

2. In 2016, Giselle had two jobs. She earned $73,440 working the first 8 months of the year at a nursing home. She switched jobs in September and began to work in a hospital, where she earned $52,211. In 2016, the maximum taxable income for Social Security was $118,500. The Social Security tax rate was 6.2%. How much OASDI tax did Giselle overpay? Round to the nearest cent.

3. Alexandra had two employers last year. Both of her employers took out OASDI tax. The OASDI percent was p and the maximum taxable OASDI income was m dollars. She earned x dollars at one job and y dollars at her second job, and $x + y > m$. Express her OASDI refund algebraically.

For Exercises 4–6 use the Social Security worksheet below.

Social Security Benefits Worksheet—Lines 20a and 20b

1. Enter the total amount from box 5 of all your Forms SSA-1099 and Forms RRB-1099. Also, enter this amount on Form 1040, line 20a ...... 1. _____
2. Enter one-half of line 1 .... 2. _____
3. Enter the total of the amounts from Form 1040, lines 7, 8a, 9a, 10 through 14, 15b, 16b, 17 through 19, and 21.. 3. _____
4. Enter the amount, if any, from Form 1040, line 8b .... 4. _____
5. Add lines 2, 3, and 4 .... 5. _____
6. Enter the total of the amounts from Form 1040, lines 23 through 32, plus any write-in adjustments you entered on the dotted line next to line 36. .... 6. _____
7. Is the amount on line 6 less than the amount on line 5?
    ☐ No. (STOP) None of your social security benefits are taxable. Enter -0- on Form 1040, line 20b.
    ☐ Yes. Subtract line 6 from line 5 .... 7. _____
8. If you are:
    • Married filing jointly, enter $32,000
    • Single, head of household, qualifying widow(er), or married filing separately and you lived apart from your spouse for all of 2008, enter $25,000 ⎫
    • Married filing separately and you lived with your spouse at any time in 20XX, skip lines 8 through 15; multiply line 7 by 85% (.85) and enter the result on line 16. Then go to line 17 ⎭ .... 8. _____
9. Is the amount on line 8 less than the amount on line 7?
    ☐ No. (STOP) None of your social security benefits are taxable. Enter -0- on Form 1040, line 20b. If you are married filing separately and you lived apart from your spouse for all of 20XX, be sure you entered "D" to the right of the word "benefits" on line 20a.
    ☐ Yes. Subtract line 8 from line 7 .... 9. _____
10. Enter: $12,000 if married filing jointly; $9,000 if single, head of household, qualifying widow(er), or married filing separately and you lived apart from your spouse for all of 2008 .. 10. _____
11. Subtract line 10 from line 9. If zero or less, enter -0- .... 11. _____
12. Enter the smaller of line 9 or line 10 .... 12. _____
13. Enter one-half of line 12 .... 13. _____
14. Enter the smaller of line 2 or line 13 .... 14. _____
15. Multiply line 11 by 85% (.85). If line 11 is zero, enter -0- .... 15. _____
16. Add lines 14 and 15... 16. _____
17. Multiply line 1 by 85% (.85) .... 17. _____
18. Taxable social security benefits. Enter the smaller of line 16 or line 17. Also enter this amount on Form 1040, line 20b .... 18. _____

4. Andrew and Julianne Franco are married and filing a joint Form 1040. Andrew is collecting Social Security, but Julianne is not. They are filling out the Social Security worksheet on page 173 so they can determine the amount of Andrew's Social Security benefits that they will pay Federal income tax on. Number a blank sheet of paper 1–18. Fill in the following lines which were taken from their tax information:

   • Line 1—Andrew received $31,555 in Social Security benefits.

   • Line 3—the total of their other sources of income is $143,677.

   • Line 4—the amount from line 8b is $502.

   • Line 6—the total to enter is $6,075.

   a. Fill in the correct entries for the rest of the lines on their Social Security worksheet.

   b. How much of Andrew's Social Security benefit must they pay Federal income tax on?

   c. How much of Andrew's Social Security benefit is not taxed?

5. Sabrina is single. She is filling out the Social Security worksheet on page 173 so she can determine the amount of her Social Security benefits that she will pay Federal income tax on. Number a blank sheet of paper 1–18. Fill in the following lines, which were taken from Sabrina's tax information:

   • Line 1 —she received $29,612 in Social Security benefits.

   • Line 3—the total of her other sources of income is $67,891.

   • Line 4—the amount from line 8b is $440.

   • Line 6—the total to enter is $3,921.

   How much of Sabrina's Social Security benefits does she have to pay tax on?

6. Mr. Stevens filled out a Social Security benefits worksheet. He received x dollars in Social Security benefits but had to pay taxes on t dollars of it.

   a. Express the fraction of his Social Security income that he had to pay tax on as a percent.

   b. Express algebraically the amount of his Social Security benefits that were not taxed.

7. Emanuel requests his annual Social Security Statement from the IRS each year. He wants to check how many Social Security credits he received for 2016. He worked all year and earned $2,962 per month. How many credits did he earn in 2016?

8. This year Phil pays m dollars for Medicare Part B coverage. He reads that this cost will go up 11.5% next year. Express the difference between this year's and next year's cost algebraically.

10-3 Pensions

Exercises

1. Dyana worked at Litton Light Manufacturing for 25 years. Her employer offers a pension benefit package with a flat benefit formula using the flat amount of $60 for each year of service to calculate her monthly pension. How much will Dyana's monthly pension benefit be?

2. Frank worked for Morton Industries for 18 years. His company offered him a flat amount of $48 for each year of service as his monthly pension package. After one year, he was notified of a 1.625% cost of living adjustment to his monthly pension benefit. Determine Frank's current monthly pension benefit.

3. Aileen worked for Penultimate Inc. for Y years. Her company offered her a flat monthly pension benefit of D dollars for each year of service. After one year in retirement, she was notified of a P percent cost of living adjustment. Write an algebraic expression that represents her current monthly pension benefit.

4. George is retiring after 30 years at Peabody Motors. The company offers him a flat yearly retirement benefit of $870 for each year of service. What will be his monthly pension?

5. Mary is retiring after working for Fashonista Limited for 21 years. The company offered her a flat retirement benefit of $50 per month for each year of the first 15 years of service and $65 per month for each year of service thereafter.

    a. What was her monthly income in the first year after retirement?

    b. What was her annual income for the first year of retirement?

    c. After one year of retirement, she received a 0.9% cost of living adjustment to her monthly pension benefit. What was her new monthly benefit?

6. Statton Realty offers their employees a flat pension plan in which a predetermined dollar amount (multiplier) is multiplied by the number of years of service to determine the monthly pension benefit using the following schedule.

YEARS EMPLOYED	MULTIPLIER
15–19	$62.50
20–25	$75.80
26+	$83.25

    After working at Statton for 25 years, Gina has decided to open her own business. What would be the difference in her monthly pension benefit if she stays for an extra year?

7. Risa's employer offers an annual pension benefit calculated by multiplying 1.875% of the career average salary times the number of years employed. Here are Risa's annual salaries over the last 15 years of employment.

56,000	56,000	57,100	57,100	58,900	58,900	58,900	62,000
65,000	65,000	66,400	66,800	66,800	68,000	68,600	

a. What is Risa's career average salary?

b. What is Risa's annual pension under this plan?

c. What percentage of her final annual salary will her annual retirement salary be? Round your answer to the nearest percent.

d. What is Risa's monthly pension benefit? Round your answer to the nearest cent.

8. Kevin is planning on retiring after 25 years of employment. For the last 3 years he has made $132,000; $135,000; and $138,000. His employer offers a defined benefit plan in which the annual pension is calculated as the product of the final 3-year average salary, the number of years of service, and a 2.25% multiplier. What will Kevin's annual pension be?

9. Depot City uses a final average formula to calculate an employee's pension benefits. The amount used in the calculations is the salary average of the final 5 years of employment. The retiree will receive an annual benefit that is equivalent to 1.2% of the final average for each year of employment. Vilma is retiring at the end of this year, after 23 years of employment at Depot City. Calculate her annual retirement pension given that her final 5 years of salaries are $63,000; $63,700; $64,000; $64,000; and $64,800.

10. Singh's employer offers a defined contribution pension plan that uses a graded 6-year vesting formula as shown here.

Years Employed	Vesting Percentage
1–2	0%
3–10	25%
10–15	45%
15–20	70%
20–35	85%
30+	100%

His employer matches $0.75 on the dollar for all of his contributions. After 16 years, Singh decides to move to a different state. His personal contributions (adjusted for losses or gains in the investment) amount to $25,000. How much of his pension will he be able to take with him?

11. Alternate Universe Inc. offers their employees P percent of the average of their last 3 years of annual salaries for each year of service to the company. Helen began working at Alternate Universe Y years ago and is now planning to retire. Her final 3 years of salaries are A, B, and C dollars. Write an algebraic expression that will represent her annual retirement benefit.

12. Richie has contributed Y dollars per month to his pension plan for each of the last R years. His employer has matched P percent of each contribution. His employer uses a graded vesting formula according to the schedule below.

Years Employed	Vesting Percentage
0	0%
1	0%
2–8	B%
9–15	C%
16–30	D%
30+	100%

Richie has decided to change jobs after R years of service where $16 \leq R \leq 30$.

a. Write an algebraic expression that represents how much he has contributed to his retirement account.

b. How much of his contributions can he take with him?

c. Write an algebraic expression that represents how much his employer has contributed to his retirement account.

d. Write an algebraic expression that represents how much of the employer contributions Richie can take with him.

13. Logan has worked at Pendleton University for the last 20 years. The university calculates their employee's pension according to the following formula.

Determine the average of the highest 5 years of annual earnings.

Determine the monthly average using the above amount.

Subtract $1,000 from that amount.

Multiply the result by 45%.

Add $500 to that result.

For each year of employment over 15 years, add 0.5% of the average monthly salary.

The final result is the monthly pension benefit.

Logan's five highest annual salaries are $73,000; $73,900; $73,900; $74,000; and $75,000. Calculate Logan's monthly pension benefit if he retires after 20 years of employment. Round any calculations to the nearest cent.

10-4 Life Insurance

Exercises

1. Mr. Kurris is 50 years old. In 4 years, his house will be paid off and his daughter will be finished with college. He wants to take out a 5-year level-term life insurance policy with a face value $750,000. The monthly premium is $61.

   a. What will be his total cost for this policy over the 5-year period?

   b. If he dies after paying for the policy for 16 months, how much will the insurance company pay his beneficiaries?

   c. If he does not die during the 5 years, how much does the insurance company make on this policy?

   d. If he dies after paying for the policy for 13 months, how much will the insurance company lose on this policy?

2. The Apple Insurance Company offers 5-year term $100,000 policies to a 46-year-old female for $516 per year. The mortality rates are shown below. Fill in the missing entries a–g in the table.

Age at Death	46	47	48	49	50	Age ≥ 51
Mortality Rate	0.0016	0.0019	0.0022	0.0027	0.0032	a.
Insurance Company Profit at End of Each Year if Purchaser Dies in That Year	b.	c.	d.	e.	f.	g.

   a. What is the expected profit for one of these policies? Round to the nearest cent.

   b. If the company sold 5,000 of the same policies to 46-year-old females, what would their expected profit be for the 5,000 policies? Round to the nearest thousand dollars.

3. Julio has a universal life insurance policy with a face value of $200,000. The current cash value of the policy is $11,560. If the premium is $102 per month, for how many months can the cash value be used to pay the premium?

4. An insurance company sells a $500,000 5-year term policy to a female. The monthly policy is m dollars. If the person dies 20 months after taking out the policy, express the insurance company's profit algebraically.

5. Mr. DiPasquale's whole life premium increased from $115 to $149 per month when he increased his face value. Find the percent increase to the nearest percent.

6. Use the mortality table below to answer parts a–f.

| Exact Age | Mortality Table for Males | | Mortality Table for Females | |
	Death Probability	Life Expectancy	Death Probability	Life Expectancy
56	0.008467	23.52	0.005148	26.94
57	0.009121	22.71	0.005627	26.07
58	0.009912	21.92	0.006166	25.22
59	0.010827	21.13	0.006765	24.37
60	0.011858	20.36	0.007445	23.53
65	0.017976	16.67	0.011511	19.50
66	0.019564	15.96	0.012572	18.72
67	0.021291	15.27	0.013772	17.95
68	0.023162	14.59	0.015130	17.19
69	0.025217	13.93	0.016651	16.45

a. What is the life expectancy for a 69-year-old female? Round to the nearest year.

b. Until what age is a 65-year-old male expected to live? Round to the nearest year.

c. If the company insures 10,000 males who are 58 years old. how many are expected to die before their 59th birthday? Round to the nearest integer.

d. Based on the table, what is the probability that a 68-year-old male will live to his 69th birthday?

7. The mortality rate for a certain female elderly age category is 0.0059. A company insures 10,000 people in this category. About how many of them will die before their next birthday?

8. Express the expected profit algebraically for the following expected value table.

Profit	a	b	c	d
Probability	0.01	0.02	0.9	0.01

9. Mr. Norton has a universal life insurance policy, and the current cash value of the policy is c. The premium is m dollars per month. He is going to use the cash value to pay for premiums as long as it can. In those months, the cash value will earn i dollars interest. Write an algebraic expression for the number of months the cash value can be used to pay the premium.

10. Use the definition of the greatest integer function to evaluate the following.

   a. [109.999]

   b. [87.007]

   c. [−50.95]

   d. $[34\frac{12}{13}]$

   e. $[\sqrt{39}]$

   f. $[\sqrt{35}]$

11. The Wonderland Miracle Carnival Company manages a game at a state fair. They charge $3 per game. Winners receive a $10 prize. The probability of winning the game is 0.15.

   a. What is the probability of losing the game?

   b. What profit does the company earn if a person wins the game?

   c. What profit does the company earn if the person loses the game?

   d. Set up a table indicating the profit and the probability of winning and losing.

   e. What is the expected profit per game?

   f. If 800 people play this game during the week-long state fair, what is the company's profit for the week?

12. Mr. Kite took out a 10-year term policy with a face-value of *f* dollars. Over the lifetime of the policy, he pays monthly payments of *m* dollars. He dies after 12 years.

   a. Express the total he paid for the policy algebraically.

   b. How much will his family receive from the insurance company?

13. Mr. Henderson takes out a term life insurance policy with a renewable annual premium. The first year premium is $350. Premiums increase by 7% each year.

   a. What will the premiums be in the second year?

   b. What will the premiums be in the third year? Round to the nearest cent.

   c. What will the premiums be in the *n*th year?

   d. Does the expression in your answer to part c model an arithmetic sequence or a geometric sequence?

10-5 Investment Diversification

Exercises

1. Rob is retiring from his teaching job. His annual pension will be $84,500, which he will receive every year until he dies. However, he has a choice to make. If he agrees to take a 10% reduction in his pension, his wife can continue to receive that annual payment even after his death, until she dies.

   a. What is the amount of the reduced annual pension?

   b. If Rob lives 10 years after retirement and receives the full $84,500 per year, how much will he have received in total?

   c. If Rob lives 20 years, and takes the reduced pension amount, and his wife lives 11 years past his death, how much will the pension have paid in total?

   d. If Rob lives 6 years after retirement and then dies, and he took the reduced pension, how much less did he receive than if he took the full $84,500 amount each year?

   e. For how many years would Rob's wife have to live to collect pension money that was more than the amount Rob sacrificed from part d?

2. The following circle graphs give the proportional breakdowns of two investors' diversified portfolios.

Diane's Portfolio

Jack's Portfolio

   a. Which investment in Diane's portfolio do you think is the most risky?

   b. Which is Jack's riskiest investment?

   c. Which portfolio do you consider to be the most risky?

   d. Out of the eight different types of investments, which one is the safest?

Financial Algebra Workbook 10-5

3. Kim is planning to set up a $90,000 investment portfolio. She plans on investing 30% into stock, 30% into bonds, 30% into collectibles, and the remainder into a 10-year certificate of deposit.

   a. How much is invested in the CD?

   b. If the CD earns 2.25% interest compounded continuously, how much will it grow to in 10 years? Round to the nearest cent.

   c. The same amount is invested in stocks as in collectibles. If the stock goes down 10%, and the collectibles gain 10% in value, what is the net gain from these two investments?

4. The Castellano family is planning to send their 1-year old twin daughters to college in 17 years. They plan on investing $4,000 each year per child to help meet their college costs.

   a. If the interest rate was 3% compounded annually, what will the value of each child's account be in 17 years? Assume the periodic, annual $4,000 deposit continues for each child.

   b. Would investing the money in a stock that had a yield of 5% earn more money than the CD? Explain.

   c. What are the advantages and disadvantages in investing the money in stock?

5. Charlotte invested $120,000 into stocks, bonds, and real estate several years ago. She diversified the investment according to the following percentages:

   Stocks: 33%

   Bonds: 42%

   Real estate: 25%

   If the stocks increase 9% in value, the bonds gain 8%, and the real estate loses 5%, what is the total monetary gain or loss from this diversified portfolio?

6. In 1985, Leslie bought a classic 1956 Chevrolet Nomad for $22,000. Over the next 31 years, he invested approximately $750 per year into restoring the car to its original condition. In 2016 he sold it for $61,000.

a. Imagine he chose not to invest in the car. Assume he invested the initial $22,000 in an account that paid an average of 9.11% interest compounded daily for the next 10 years. How much would that grow to in the 10 years? Round to the nearest hundred dollars.

b. Interest rates started to fall in the 1990s. Imagine he took the money the account had earned in part a (after rounding) and invested it in a CD that paid an average of 4% compounded daily for the remaining 21 years. How much would that grow to by 2016? Round to the nearest hundred dollars.

c. If he deposited $750 each year into an account that paid 4.09% compounded annually, how much would be in that account after the 31 years? Round to the nearest hundred dollars.

d. How much of a gain would the three accounts from parts a, b, and c make in the 31 years, to the nearest hundred dollars?

e. How much did he invest in the Nomad?

f. How much did he gain on the Nomad investment?

g. Which investment was more conservative?

11-1 | Utility Expenses

Exercises

1. LED light bulbs are replacing incandescent light bulbs because over 90% of the energy consumed by an incandescent bulb goes in to producing heat, not light. The 14-watt LightKing LED costs $1.32 in electricity per year. The 60-watt LightKing incandescent bulb gives the same amount of light but costs $6.09 in electricity per year. How much could be saved per year by using 25 of the LED bulbs in a house?

2. The Ricardo household used *w* cubic feet of water during a summer month. Express the number of ccf of water they used algebraically.

3. Mrs. Zorn works for a utility company and is reading the electric meter for a local pizza place, which is shown below.

   How many kWh of electricity are indicated by the dials?

4. A certain guitar amplifier requires 200 watts when it is being used. How much would it cost to run for 55 minutes, at a cost of $0.11 per kWh? Round to the nearest cent.

5. The dials shown below are from a natural gas meter and display the number of ccf used. How many ccf are indicated by the dials?

6. The Simpsons' previous water bill showed a meter reading of 433 ccf. Below is their meter's current reading. At a cost of $0.91 per ccf, what should their next water bill be?

7. The Robinsons' old dryer cost them $455 per year to run. The new one they purchased for $940 will save them 18% annually in energy costs to run it. In how many years will it pay for itself?

8. An appliance uses *w* watts to run. If you run it for *h* hours, and the cost per kilowatt-hour is *c*, express the cost of running the appliance per kwh algebraically.

9. The Nesmiths' old clothes washer costs *c* dollars to run for a year. They replace it with a new energy-efficient washer that costs *w* dollars, but saves *p* percent per year in energy usage. How many years will it take for the washer to pay for itself? Express your answer algebraically using the greatest integer function.

10. Two years ago the Lange family used $3,250 worth of electricity. Last year they switched to balanced billing.

    a. What was their monthly payment last year under balanced billing? Round to the nearest cent.

    b. During last year, they actually used $3,766 of electricity and their balanced billing payments were not enough to pay for their electrical usage. They had to pay the difference at the end of the year. How much did they owe the utility company?

11. Last winter, the Kranepool family used 431 gallons of heating oil at a price of $4.12 per gallon. If the price increases 8.25% next year, what will their approximate heating expense be for the year? Round to the nearest ten dollars.

12. A typical light bulb requires 60 watts to run when it is turned on. If a light fixture requires three of these bulbs, and the light is left on unnecessarily for four hours per day, how many kWh of electricity are wasted each year?

13. Mr. Denton's last water bill was for $109.56. The previous reading was 1,209 ccf and the present reading was 1,417 ccf. What does his water company charge for 100 cubic feet of water? Round to the nearest cent.

14. The Manilow family paid their electric bill using balanced billing all last year. The monthly payment was *m* dollars. At the end of the year, the electric company told them they used more electricity than they were billed for, and they owed *d* dollars. Express the value of the electricity used by the Manilows last year algebraically.

15. A water bill listed a previous reading of 4,501 ccf and a present reading of 4,971 ccf. The water company charges $0.86 per ccf of water. What should have been charged on this water bill?

16. One watt hour is equivalent to 3.413 BTUs per hour.

    a. If an air conditioner is rated at 10,000 BTU, how many watts does it require per hour? Round to the nearest hundred watts.

    b. Express your answer to part a in kWh.

    c. If you run an air conditioner for 15 hours per day, and electricity costs $0.12 per kWh, estimate the cost of running the air conditioner for 15 hours on 60 summer days. Round to the nearest dollar.

17. The following box-and-whisker plot gives the monthly costs of electricity for the Sharkey household for the year.

$112 $398

          $166 $202 $325

    a. How many months was the bill $202 or less?

    b. How many months had bills greater than or equal to $166?

    c. If they have gas heat, and they live in Virginia, which month do you think had the $398 bill? Explain your reasoning.

    d. If they have electric heat, and they live in Minnesota, which month do you think had the $398 bill? Explain.

18. The Lennon family used *x* dollars worth of electricity two years ago and then switched to balanced billing.

    a. Express the amount of their monthly balanced billing payment algebraically.

    b. Last year, they underpaid their bill and were charged *c* dollars at the end of the year to make up for the underpaid charges. Express the amount of this year's balanced billing monthly payment algebraically, if it was based on last year's usage.

  19. How many cubic feet are represented by the following water meter?

20. It has been reported that an electric clothes dryer can account for about 12% of the electricity used in an average household. With that much electrical consumption in mind, it is important to choose wisely when making a dryer purchase. WestEnd Electric manufactures two different types of clothes dryers. The Energy Dry model costs $700 and is expected to use $140 per year in electricity. The Vista model costs $400 and is expected to use $180 per year in electricity.

    a. Set up a cost function, $E(x)$, to represent the cost of owning and operating the Energy Dry model over a period of x years.

    b. Set up a cost function, $V(x)$, to represent the cost of owning and operating the Vista model over a period of x years.

    c. Set up an average yearly cost rational function, $A(x)$, for the Energy Dry model.

    d. Set up an average yearly cost rational function, $B(x)$, for the Vista model.

    e. Graph both average yearly cost functions $A(x)$ and $B(x)$ on the same axes. Interpret the graphs in terms of the average yearly cost for owning and operating each dryer.

Name _____   Date _____

11-2 Electronic Utilities

Exercises

1. Micaela's cell phone plan has a monthly fee of $87, which includes unlimited free text messages and phone calls, and 4GB of data. Each extra GB of data costs $15. Find the cost of a month in which Micaela uses 5.2GB of data.

2. A wireless phone company's *Call-All* phone plan has a basic charge per month, which includes a certain amount of gigabytes. There is a charge for each additional gigabyte. The split function below gives the price $c(g)$ of using gigabytes for data. Fractions of a gigabyte are charged as if they were a full GB.

$$c(g) = \begin{cases} 59 & \text{when } g \le 6 \\ 59+16.50(g-6) & \text{when } g > 6 \text{ and } g \text{ is an integer} \\ 59+16.50[g-6]+1 & \text{when } g > 6 \text{ and } g \text{ is not an integer} \end{cases}$$

   a. Describe the cost of the *Call-All* phone plan by interpreting the split function.

   b. Find the monthly cost of the *Call-All* phone plan for someone that used 7.7GB.

3. The Tech-N-Text phone company charges $48 for unlimited texting per month, or $0.16 per text message sent or received. For what amount of text messages would the unlimited plan cost the same as the per-text plan?

4. Next-Text charges $19 for a pre-paid phone card with 250 text messages included. If the customer goes over the 250 messages, the cost is $0.12 per text message. They have an unlimited plan, which costs $45 per month.

   a. If t represents the number of text messages, and $c(t)$ represents the cost of the messages, express $c(t)$ as a split function in terms of t.

   b. Graph the function from part a. What are the coordinates of the cusp?

   c. On the same axes, graph the function $c(t) = 45$, which represents the cost under the unlimited plan.

   d. Find the coordinates of the point of intersection of the two graphs. Round to the nearest hundredth.

   e. For what number of text messages are the costs of the two different plans the same? Round to the nearest integer.

5. A cable TV provider charges Nina $99 per month for three services—Internet, land-line phone, and cable television. In addition, Nina's monthly bill for cell phone calls and text messages averages $59.70 per month. What is her average cost per day for these four services? Round to the nearest dollar.

6. Randi, a college student, is taking a semester abroad. She purchases a one-time use, 90-day international cell phone plan. There is a one-time fee of $85 and it includes 400MB of data usage. Each extra MB, or part thereof, of data costs $0.21. Express the cost of this plan as a piecewise function.

7. Examine the following split function which gives the cost $c(t)$ of t text messages per month.

$$c(t) = \begin{cases} w & \text{when } t \leq r \\ w + k(t-r) & \text{when } t > r \end{cases}$$

   a. If Sophie had r text messages, what is the cost for the month?

   b. Is the cost of $2r$ text messages double the cost of r text messages? Explain.

8. Eleni uses 6.8 GB of data per month and plan, which costs $70 per month and includes 4GB of data. Each extra GB is $x. Express algebraically the average cost per GB of using this plan when 6.8GB of data are used.

9. The Super Vision cable TV/Internet/phone provider advertises a flat $100 monthly fee for all three services for a new customer. The rate is guaranteed for 5 years. Cable Zone normally charges $46 for monthly home phone service, $36 for monthly Internet service, and $56 for monthly cable television.

   a. How much could a customer save during the first year by switching from Cable Zone to Super Vision?

   b. Super Vision raises the rates 23% after a new customer's first year, how much will a customer who switched from Super Vision save in the second year?

   c. If Super Vision raises the rates 18% for the third year compared to the second year, which company is cheaper for the third year?

10. A phone company set the following rate schedule for an m-minute call from any of its airport pay phones.

$$c(m) = \begin{cases} 0.95 & \text{when } m \leq 6 \\ 0.95 + 0.24(m-6) & \text{when } m > 6 \text{ and } m \text{ is an integer} \\ 0.95 + 0.24([m-6]+1) & \text{when } m > 6 \text{ and } m \text{ is not an integer} \end{cases}$$

What is the difference in the costs of a $10\frac{1}{2}$ minute call compared to an 11-minute call?

11. Tay wants to purchase a new cell phone and change her service provider to WestCell. She can either buy the phone through WestCell or purchase the phone on her own at an electronics store or website. If she buys the phone through WestCell, they are offering her a reduced price in which they subsidize the difference between the discounted and regular price of the phone. She will also need to purchase the service plan through them. If she buys the phone on her own, she will then need to shop around for a service plan provider. Tay found the following information on both types of plans for the latest version of a smart phone she wishes to purchase:

Subsidized by WestCell: $250 for the phone plus $80 per month for unlimited talk and text and 3 GB of data.

Unsubsidized: $700 for the phone purchased at Great Buy plus a monthly $60 service plan through the provider RingZ for unlimited talk and text and 3 GB of data.

Create an average cost rational function for each possibility. Graph the functions and interpret the intersection point.

11-3 Charting a Budget

Exercises

1. Construct a pie chart to represent the percentages that Theo has determined as his monthly expenses.

   Household: 32%

   Education: 23%

   Transportation: 16%

   Health: 12%

   Savings: 9%

   Miscellaneous: 8%

2. Identify the approximate percentages allocated for each of the categories in the pie chart.

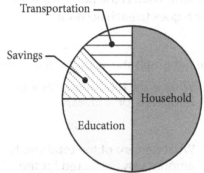

Budget Categories

3. The pie chart shows Winnie's monthly budget allocation of $4,000. Construct a bar graph using this information. Use the categories for the horizontal axis and the budgeted amounts for the vertical axis.

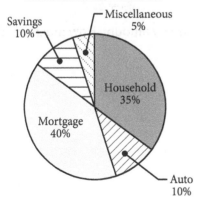

Winnie's Monthly Budget

4. Create a year-long budget matrix to chart the following medical related expenses: Healthcare premium: $120 twice a month; Prescriptions: $80 monthly; Physical exams: $225 semiannually; Dental insurance: $60 quarterly; Eyeglasses: $300 annually (June); Physical Therapy: $100 (bimonthly beginning in February).

5. Vinny's financial budget is as follows: The percentage budgeted for his retirement account is three times the percentage for his savings account. The percentage budgeted for his savings account is one-fourth the percentage budgeted for his checking account. The percentage budgeted for his stock investments is two-thirds the percentage budgeted for his retirement account. What is the percentage for checking? If $1,200 is budgeted for the entire category, how much goes to each account?

6. The bar graph shows budgeted monthly utility expenses for a 1-year period.

   a. What is the total annual amount budgeted for utilities?

   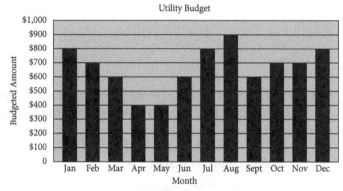

   b. What percent of the total yearly amount was budgeted for the months of June–September?

   c. The homeowners replaced their furnace with a more energy efficient one. They were told that they could decrease their utility budget for the upcoming month of January by 20% from the previous January amount. How much will they budget for utilities in January?

7. Construct a bar graph for the September budget category "Personal Items" using the following amounts: Hair cut $20, Clothing purchases $60, Books $20, Newspapers/Magazines $65, Online Subscriptions $30, Gifts $80, Donations $40, and Other $50.

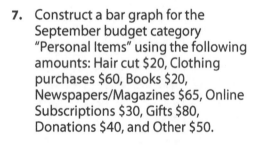

Name _____ Date _____

8. Tina's primary source of income pays a fixed amount and her secondary source of income varies monthly. In preparing her budget for the year, she has entered the amounts she has agreed to be paid when working her second job in the given months. She also has income from interest-bearing savings accounts and stock dividends. She used actual amounts from the previous year to set up this budget for the upcoming year.

	Jan	Feb	Mar	Apr	May	Jun	Jul	Aug	Sep	Oct	Nov	Dec
Primary Source	7,500	7,500	7,500	7,500	7,500	7,500	7,500	7,500	7,500	7,500	7,500	7,500
Secondary Source	1,300	1,800			1,500		2,500	1,500		2,200	2,000	4,000
Interest			250			280			310			350
Dividends			600			150			150			150
Other						3,000						3,000

a. What is her budgeted income for each month?

b. Construct a line graph of this budget.

c. Determine the average monthly income to the nearest dollar.

d. Draw a horizontal line on your graph representing that amount. What months fell below the average?

9. Aida created a double bar graph to illustrate the actual amounts spent this year for household expenses and the budgeted amounts for the following year. The following year's amounts reflect a 5% increase over the COLA. For June, the actual amount is $1,200 and the budgeted amount for Year 2 is $1,320.

a. What was the cost of living adjustment that Aida used to get the budgeted amounts?

b. Determine the budgeted amount for January of Year 2.

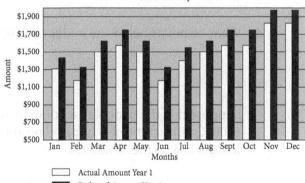

c. The August actual amount was the exact amount Aida had budgeted for. This actual amount reflected an 8% increase over the previous year's actual amount for August. What was the previous year's actual amount for August rounded to the nearest dollar?

10. Under his "Garden Project" budget category, Steve has allocated $480 for two types of ground cover material. He can purchase "Premium Landscaping Rock" for $8 per bag or "Cedar Mulch Chips" for $4 per bag. Both bags cover the same square footage. He wants to buy a combination of both and stay within his budget.

   a. Determine a budget line equation for this situation.

   b. Graph the budget line depicting the different combinations of rock bags and cedar bags that Steve can purchase while still remaining within his budget.

   c. Name a combination of rock bags and cedar bags that will allow him to meet his budget exactly.

   d. Name a combination of rock bags and cedar bags that will keep him under budget.

   e. Name a combination of rock bags and cedar bags that will cause him to be over budget.

11. Jen's employer gives her a budget of $500 per month for transportation. She has determined that the cost of using a car-share vehicle is $20 per round trip and the cost of using a limousine service is $25 per round-trip. She wants to stay within the budget for these trips by using a combination of both.

   a. Write a budget line equation for this situation.

   b. Construct the budget line graph that models this situation.

   c. What do the points on the budget line represent?

   d. What do points below the budget line represent?

   e. Suppose that the budgeted amount increases to $600. Construct the new budget line and the old budget line on the same axes.

   f. What does the region in between the two lines represent?

11-4 Cash Flow and Budgeting

Exercises

1. Below is a budget table listing the actual amounts that were spent for each of the utilities categories during the first 6 months of the year. Freda wants to alter her current budget during the last 6 months and use the average of the actual amounts in each category. Complete the table with the average amount for each category.

	Jan	Feb	Mar	Apr	May	Jun	Average
Electric	110	140	135	135	130	140	a.
Water	90	85	76	80	85	85	b.
Cable	110	105	115	120	115	115	c.
Cell phone	80	90	120	140	110	110	d.
Land-line phone	40	35	35	35	40	45	e.
Sanitation	60	70	70	60	60	60	f.
Heating Fuel	450	520	500	300	100	50	g.

2. Quincy Gallois is single and owns a co-op. He has calculated the following assets and liabilities. Find Quincy's net worth.

ASSETS

Current value of the co-op: $180,000

Current value of car: $12,500

Checking account balance: $1,300

Combined savings: $18,000

Balance in retirement account: $30,000

Current value of owned electronics: $20,000

LIABILITIES

Remaining balance on mortgage: $120,000

Remaining balance on personal loan: $4,600

Combined credit card debt: $23,000

3. Celine's monthly liabilities and assets are given in the table. Determine Celine's debt-to-income ratio. Express that ratio as a percent.

Monthly Liabilities (Debt)		Monthly Pre-Tax Assets (Income)	
Mortgage Payment	$2,560	Gross Salary	$6,900
Student Loan Payment	$350	Income from Rental Property	$900
Minimum Credit Card Payment	$50		
Car Loan Payment	$120		

Name _____ Date _____

Use the following financial information for Bill Marshall to answer Exercises 4–8.

Financial Report			
Income			
Architect, monthly after-tax income: $8,000			
Consultant, monthly after-tax income: $2,000			
Monthly Expenses			
Rent	$2,800	Groceries	$220
Car loan	$200	Personal loan	$300
Electricity	$80	Land line phone	$40
Sanitation	$50	Auto insurance	$300
Cable/Internet	$100	Savings	$600
Dining out	$200	College loan	$260
Gasoline	$180	Cell phone	$90
Water	$40	Medical insurance	$60
Renter's insurance	$50	Entertainment	$200
Credit card debt	$500		

Non-Monthly Expenses
Medical: $300 in June, $160 in October
Auto-related: $1,200 in July
Home-related: $300 in March, $600 in September
Life insurance: $200 in February, June, October
Computer: $3,000 in January
Vacation: $1,200 in August
Gifts: $500 in May, $400 in December
Contributions: $20 each week of the year
Repairs: $1,500 in November

4. The Consumer Credit Counseling Service suggests that the monthly food budget be no greater than 30% of the income.

   a. What is Bill's total monthly food bill including dining out?

   b. What percent of his income is spent on food?

5. Examine Bill's non-monthly expenses. Find the total and the monthly average of these expenses.

6. Use the cash flow to construct a cash flow plan for Bill. What is his monthly cash flow?

INCOME				
Primary Employment				
Secondary Employment				
Other Employment				
TOTAL INCOME				
FIXED EXPENSES		**NON-MONTHLY EXPENSES (per year)**		
Rent/Mortgage		Medical/Dental		
Car Loan Payment		Auto-related		
Education Loan Payment		Home-related		
Personal Loan Payment		Life Insurance		
Health Insurance Premium		Computer		
Cable/Internet		Vacation		
Car Insurance Premium		Gifts		
Homeowner's/Renter's Insurance		Contributions		
TOTAL FIXED EXPENSES		Repairs		
		TOTAL NON-MONTHLY EXPENSES (per year)		
		TOTAL NON-MONTHLY EXPENSES (per month)		
VARIABLE EXPENSES				
Groceries (food)				
Dining Out				
Fuel (car)				
Cell Phone				
Land Line Phone				
Electricity				
Water				
Sanitation				
Entertainment				
Savings				
Debt Reduction				
Other				
TOTAL VARIABLE EXPENSES				
TOTAL EXPENSES				
MONTHLY CASH FLOW				

7. Create a frequency budget for Bill. Although his food, fuel, dining out, and entertainment expenses were listed as monthly for the cash flow, they should be considered as weekly expenses here. To find the weekly amount, multiply the monthly amount by 12 and then divide by 52 weeks. Round your answer up to the nearest dollar. Combine electricity, water, and sanitation under the "utilities" category. Any categories not mentioned in the template belong in the appropriate "other" section. What is Bill's surplus or deficit for the year?

AFTER TAX INCOME CATEGORIES	INCOME AMOUNTS	FREQUENCY	ANNUAL AMOUNT
Primary Employment			
Secondary Employment			
Interest			
Dividends			
Other Income			
TOTAL INCOME			
WEEKLY EXPENSES	**EXPENSE AMOUNTS**		
Food			
Personal Transportation			
Public Transportation			
Household			
Childcare			
Dining Out			
Entertainment			
Other (contributions)			
TOTAL WEEKLY EXPENSES			
MONTHLY EXPENSES			
Rent			
Utilities			
Land Line/Cellular Telephone			
Car Loan			
Education Loan			
Personal Loan			
Health Insurance			
Cable/Internet			
Car Insurance			
Renter's Insurance			
Savings			
Debt Reduction			
(continued on next page)			

(continued from previous page)			
Other			
TOTAL MONTHLY EXPENSES			
OTHER FREQUENCY EXPENSES			
Medical/Dental			
Auto-related			
Home-related			
Life insurance			
Computer purchase			
Vacation			
Gifts			
Contributions			
Repairs			
Taxes			
Other			
TOTAL OTHER FREQUENCY EXPENSES			
TOTAL EXPENSES			
ANNUAL SURPLUS or DEFICIT			

Name _____ Date _____

8. Use the year-long budget template on the next two pages to create a year-long budget for Bill.

	Jan	Feb	Mar	Apr	May	Jun	Jul	Aug	Sep	Oct	Nov	Dec
INCOME												
Primary Employment												
Secondary Employment												
Other Employment												
TOTAL INCOME												
FIXED EXPENSES												
Rent/Mortgage												
Car Loan Payment												
Education Loan Payment												
Personal Loan Payment												
Health Insurance Premium												
Cable/Internet												
Car Insurance Premium												
Homeowner's/Renter's Insurance												
Life Insurance												
VARIABLE EXPENSES												
Groceries (food)												
Dining Out												
Fuel (car)												
Cell Phone												
(continued on next page)												

(continued from previous page)	Jan	Feb	Mar	Apr	May	Jun	Jul	Aug	Sep	Oct	Nov	Dec
Land Line Phone												
Electricity												
Water												
Sanitation												
Medical/Dental												
Auto-related												
Home-related												
Vacation												
Gifts												
Contributions												
Repairs												
Entertainment												
Savings												
Debt Reduction												
Computer												
Other												
TOTAL EXPENSES												

11-5 Budget Matrices

Exercises

1. Examine these three matrices:

$$X = \begin{bmatrix} 2 & 5 & -1 \\ 3 & 0 & 4 \\ 6 & 1 & 1 \end{bmatrix}, \qquad Y = \begin{bmatrix} 4.5 & 10 \\ 8 & 9 \\ -7 & 3 \end{bmatrix}, \qquad Z = \begin{bmatrix} 7 & -2.5 & 6 \\ 3 & 4 & -5 \\ 5.2 & -1 & 0 \end{bmatrix}$$

   a. What are the dimensions of Y?

   b. List the elements of Z with their location symbols.

Determine each matrix in c–i.

   c. $X + Z$

   d. $Z + X$

   e. $X - Z$

   f. $Z - X$

   g. $3Z$

   h. $0.5X$

   i. XY

2. Examine this portion of Chase's budget chart for April, May, and June:

Variable Expenses	April	May	June
Groceries	$800	$600	$750
Dining Out	250	100	50
Fuel (Car)	350	350	350
Cell Phone	90	70	85
Electricity	50	75	60
Water	40	40	40

Let matrix C be a 6 by 3 matrix whose elements are the entries in the budget chart above.

a. What is the value of the element $C_{2,3}$?

b. What is the value of the element $C_{5,1}$?

c. What is the value of the element $C_{6,2}$?

d. Which element has a value of 60?

e. Which element has a value of 90?

f. What would happen to each of the elements in the matrix $4C$?

3. What are the dimensions of each of the following matrices?

a.
$$\begin{bmatrix} 1 \\ 3 \end{bmatrix}$$

b. $\begin{bmatrix} -0.5 \end{bmatrix}$

c. $\begin{bmatrix} 6 & 0 & 7 & 112 & 19 & 5 \end{bmatrix}$

d.
$$\begin{bmatrix} 2 & 1 & 0 & 0 \\ 0 & 1 & 0 & 1 \\ 0 & 0 & 1 & 2 \end{bmatrix}$$

e.
$$\begin{bmatrix} 0.08 & 11 & 0 & 0.6 \\ 3 & 1 & 4 & 6 \\ \frac{1}{2} & \frac{1}{4} & \frac{3}{8} & \frac{4}{5} \\ 0.7 & 0.77 & 0.725 & 0.7 \\ 0 & 1 & 1 & 0 \end{bmatrix}$$

4. Given $A = \begin{bmatrix} 1 & 2 & 3 & 4 \\ 4 & 3 & 2 & 1 \end{bmatrix}$, $B = \begin{bmatrix} 0 & 1 \\ 1 & 0 \\ 1 & 1 \end{bmatrix}$, $C = \begin{bmatrix} 8 & 8 & 2 \\ 2 & 8 & 8 \end{bmatrix}$, $D = \begin{bmatrix} -0.5 & 0.3 \end{bmatrix}$

$E = \begin{bmatrix} 1 & 2 & 3 \\ 4 & 5 & 6 \end{bmatrix}$, $F = \begin{bmatrix} 0 & 7 & 0 \\ 6 & 4 & 2 \\ 9 & 2 & 2 \end{bmatrix}$, $G = \begin{bmatrix} 1 & 0 \\ 7 & 8 \\ 2 & 5 \end{bmatrix}$, $H = \begin{bmatrix} 9 & 8 \\ -9 & -8 \end{bmatrix}$

Which of the following matrix operations are defined?

a. $A + B$ b. $E + H$ c. $4C - 3E$ d. $E + G$ e. BC f. AF g. A^2 h. F^2

5. Mason's Internet supplier is making a gradual increase in fees from January to June according to the following plan:

January $80

February 0.5% increase

March 0.65 % increase from January

April 0.8% increase from January

May 0.9% increase from January

June 1% increase from January.

Let matrix A be the matrix of 6 months of fees before the increase.

$A = \begin{bmatrix} 80 & 80 & 80 & 80 & 80 & 80 \end{bmatrix}$

Let matrix B be the percent increase matrix with entries written as equivalent decimals.

$B = \begin{bmatrix} 1 \\ 1.005 \\ 1.0065 \\ 1.008 \\ 1.009 \\ 1.01 \end{bmatrix}$

Calculate AB. What does that matrix represent?

6. Zeb and Avril are married computer specialists. Their job requires them to take graduate school computer science courses to keep their skills fresh. They keep individual budget charts of their education-related expenses for tax purposes. The charts below are for the spring semester.

Zeb's Expenses

Category	February	March	April	May
Tuition	$280	$280	$280	$280
Supplies	60	60	0	0
Transportation	90	90	90	90
Downloads	120	0	50	0
Fees	40	40	40	40

Avril's Expenses

Category	February	March	April	May
Tuition	$400	$400	$400	$400
Supplies	50	100	0	0
Transportation	150	200	150	150
Downloads	300	0	0	0
Fees	70	70	70	70

a. Let matrix Z be a 5 by 4 matrix consisting of Zeb's expenses. Write matrix Z.

b. Let matrix A be a 5 by 4 matrix consisting of Avril's expenses. Write matrix A.

c. What would $A + Z$ represent? Write matrix $A + Z$, their combined education-related expenses.

7. Use Avril's matrix A from exercise #6b above. Avril knows that in the next 4-month semester her tuition will decrease by 10%, her supplies will decrease by 5%, her transportation will remain the same, her download costs will remain the same, and her fees will increase by 10%. Write a 1 by 5 percent change matrix that could be multiplied times matrix A to yield a 1 by 4 matrix that will list the total education-related expenses for each month. Then determine that final matrix.

8. Determine the values of a, b, and c in the following matrix equation.

$$X = \begin{bmatrix} 3 & a & 2 \\ -1 & 4 & c \\ 5 & 6 & -7 \end{bmatrix} \quad Y = \begin{bmatrix} 1 & 6 \\ 5 & 0 \\ 8 & -2 \end{bmatrix}$$

$$XY = \begin{bmatrix} 24 & b \\ 51 & -14 \\ -21 & 44 \end{bmatrix}$$

9. The Verrazano High School Ski Club is having a fundraiser. They are selling school water bottles, ski caps, and stuffed mascots to make enough money to go to the ski competition in December. The following matrix gives the sales numbers for September, October, and November.

	September	October	November
Water Bottles	200	150	250
Ski Caps	180	100	150
Mascots	90	80	120

The profit that the club makes on each item sold is given here:

Water Bottles	Ski Caps	Mascots
$2.00	$4.00	$3.25

Find the product of the two matrices. Explain what the product represents.

For Practice

For Practice

For Practice

For Practice

For Practice

For Practice

For Practice

For Practice

For Practice

For Practice